FROM ST. LOUIS TO COOPERSTOWN

BASEBALL LEGENDS BORN AND MADE IN THE GATEWAY CITY

BY ED WHEATLEY

Reedy Press
PO Box 5131
St. Louis, MO, 63139, USA
reedypress.com

Cover images (left to right and top to bottom): Getty Images, Getty Images, Getty Images, Getty Images, Getty Images, Getty Images, Getty Images, Getty Images, Getty Images, Wikimedia Commons, Getty Images, Wikimedia Commons, Public Domain, Getty Images, Public Domain, Public Domain, Getty Images, Getty Images, Getty Images, Wikimedia Commons, Wikimedia Commons, Getty Images, Getty Images, Public Domain.

Wikipedia image credits: page 82: Johnmaxmena; page 92: UCinternational; page 93: SD Dirk; page 97: Keith Allison.

Unless otherwise noted, all photos are courtesy of the author or believed to be in the public domain.

LOC: 2024949291
ISBN: 9781681065786

Printed in the United States of America
25 26 27 28 29 5 4 3 2 1

Table of Contents

Rube Wadell
Wikimedia Commons

Bruce Sutter
Getty Images

Oscar Charleston
Wikimedia Commons

Sportsman's Park, 1946 World Series
Missouri Historical Society, St. Louis

Sportsman's Park, 1964 World Series
Missouri Historical Society, St. Louis

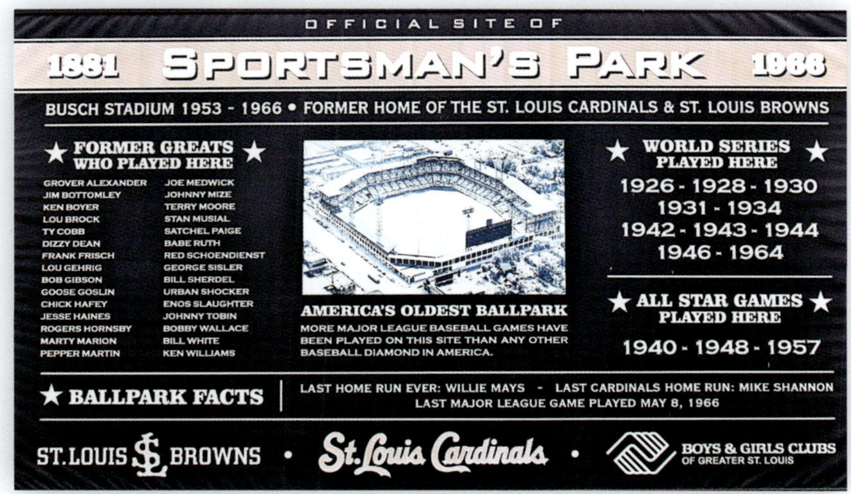

Introduction: Welcome to Baseball in St. Louis

St. Louis's love affair with baseball is more than just a day at the ballpark. It's a cornerstone of the city's history. It brings St. Louisans together to "root, root, root, for the home team!" Along the way they root for their favorite players, including many of the best in the game who spent time playing for or growing up in St. Louis. This anthology tells the story of those men inducted into the National Baseball Hall of Fame in Cooperstown and their ties to St. Louis.

Three hundred and forty-six individuals have been inducted into Baseball's Hall of Fame, the highest honor that can be bestowed upon a player, manager, or executive in the game of baseball. The inductees include 245 former major league players and an additional 28 men who played in the Negro Leagues at a time when they were not allowed to play on a major league team. Twenty-three men have also been inducted as managers and another ten who were umpires. The Hall also recognizes 40 inductees for their off-the-field contributions to the game as pioneers, executives, or organizers. Of these 40, eight men and one woman (Effa Manley) were inducted for their contributions to the Negro Leagues.

Bob Gibson
Getty Images

While numbers have always been an important part of baseball, these Hall of Fame numbers reflect an important piece of St. Louis's baseball history. Since the first honorees were selected 89 years ago in 1936, there have been 81 induction classes along with eight years when no one was selected. Inductees with ties to St. Louis have been included in 54 percent of those 81 induction classes.

It's quite a statement about St. Louis baseball when over half of the Hall of Fame's induction classes have included at least one individual tied to the city. These 44 induction classes have included 49 MLB players, six Negro League players, 12 managers, and four executives. In total St. St. Louis's ties to the Hall of Fame represent 21 percent of all inductees. Simply put, one of every five inductees has roots planted in St. Louis.

Not only do these pages provide the biographies and stats of these Hall of Famers, but the players are ordered by their year of induction to document an intertwining history of the players with each other and the teams they played on, as well as the changes that have taken place within the game of baseball. Some players spent their whole career in St. Louis, and for others their time in the Gateway City was short. One future Hall of Famer's big-

Mark Engelhardt Collection

league playing career in St. Louis lasted only two innings in just one game. It's no surprise that these stories reference so many World Series. Great teams are made by great players and managers. And St. Louis has seen many of the game's best while claiming the second-most World Series Championships in major league history. How much of this success is due to 52 percent of all inducted managers having ties to St. Louis? The statistics alone are a reflection of St. Louis's baseball and are worthy of a full-length "hot stove" discussion.

But another factor contributing to St. Louis's special relationship with baseball is the city's supportive and intelligent fans. Beyond the events on the field of play, St. Louisans have been nurtured by the region's award-winning broadcasters and sportswriters, many of whom are honored in their respective wings of the Baseball Hall of Fame. Their stories are included within this collection as well. As each new season comes and goes, St. Louisans root for their home team with hopes of another pennant and cheer its players hoping a special few may one day become members of the National Baseball Hall of Fame.

Player statistics have been the holy grail of baseball analytics and hot stove debates of a player's worth ever since the game was first played. During the past century, research and technology have provided insights and adjustments to individual record books. While many reputable sources of players statistics exist, a triangulation review of the data points often turns out discrepancies between the sources. This is even more pronounced when studying the individual results of players from the Negro Leagues, where data was not fully recorded and validated with the same due diligence as in Major League Baseball. Within these pages, we have chosen to use the statistical summary of individual results using BaseballReference.com as the definitive source across these pages.

Baseball analytics have played an increasing role within baseball over the past decade. WAR and the Slash Line are the two most prominent metrics used to assess a player's value. They have been included in the player's biographical information to offer statistical comparisons across all generations of the game. All players have a WAR calculated for them. WAR measures a player's value in all facets of the game by deciphering how many more wins he's worth than a replacement-level player at his same position (e.g., a Minor League replacement or a readily available fill-in free agent). For the record, Babe Ruth has the highest career WAR in Major League Baseball history at 182.6. Walter Johnson has the second highest and highest as a pitcher at 166.9. The Slash Line is applied only to offensive players and consists of three stats separated by forward slashes: a player's batting average / on-base percentage / slugging percentage. This metric has become a recent standard since reviewing one statistic at a time doesn't always paint the whole offense capabilities of a given player.

St. Louis Browns baseball player at bat in Sportsman's Park
Missouri Historical Society, St. Louis

Sportsman's Park Postcard

Missouri Historical Society, St. Louis

Ozzie Smith
Getty Images

MIssouri Historical Society, St. Louis

John McGraw
Library of Congress

Miller Higgins
Library of Congress

Major Leaguers: Players from the St. Louis Cardinals Franchise

The following section highlights those 54 men inducted into the National Baseball Hall of Fame who were at one point in their career a member of today's St. Louis Cardinals franchise. Baseball fans rightly expect that there to be a significant number of Cardinals inducted into the Hall of Fame due to the team's longevity and success. Only the fabled New York Yankees have won more World Series Championships (27) than the St. Louis Cardinals (11). The Cardinal franchise can, however, add one more championship to their Fall Classic collection if they include their 1886 win in the Championship Series, held from 1882 to 1891 and played between the champions of the American Association (A.A.) and National League (N.L.)—a predecessor to today's World Series. The St. Louis A.A. team, known as the St. Louis Browns, was the league's premier team (four-time winners from 1885 to 1888) and the only A.A. team to defeat an N.L. team during the decade-long existence of the Championship Series. Ironically, they defeated the Chicago White Stockings (later renamed the Cubs} to start one of baseball's longest and greatest city rivalries.

Several players and managers of this A.A. St. Louis Browns team are inductees in the Hall of Fame and are included in these pages as members of the Cardinals franchise. This Browns team has no ties or lineage to the Browns that joined the American League (A.L.) in 1902. These A.A. Browns joined the N.L. in 1892 and carried the Browns name until 1898, creating some confusion over the moniker "St. Louis Browns" for students of baseball history. The franchise would then change its name in 1899 to the Perfectos prior to once more changing its name to the Cardinals in 1900 after their adoption of that lovely shade of cardinal red on their uniforms.

To complicate matters a little more, there was another iteration of a St. Louis team with a "Browns" reference. The St. Louis Brown Stockings were an inaugural N.L. team in 1876. They lasted just two seasons before being expelled due to gambling issues. That team had been a member of the National Association for one year in 1875 before their inclusion in that first class of the N.L. Cardinal franchise Hall of Famer Pud Galvin was a member of this team and also played for the 1892 Browns team during its first season in the N.L.

Eighteen of these 54 inductees' careers were primarily spent within the Cardinals franchise. Others only played a season or two and one future Hall of Famer played only three innings of one game with the Redbirds. Yet no matter how many games or innings they played, they remain part of one of baseball's greatest franchises. Here are their stories.

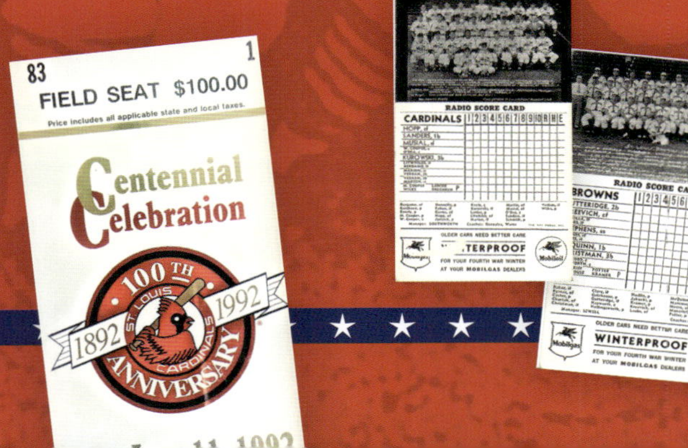

John McGraw

Baseball fans associate John McGraw with his years managing the New York Giants. Few are even aware of his lone season in St. Louis. McGraw retired in 1932 as the N.L.'s winningest manager to date. Seldom are there discussions of his 17-year career as one of baseball's best leadoff hitters. McGraw batted .334 to go along with a career on base percentage of .4657—surpassed only by Ted Williams (.4817) and Babe Ruth (.4734). For nine straight years McGraw hit over .320 and twice led the league in runs and walks while adding 436 career stolen bases to his resume. But it was not his playing career that got McGraw to Cooperstown; it was his 33 seasons as one of the game's best managers that put him in the Hall of Fame's second induction class in 1937.

McGraw's St. Louis connection occurred in just one of the 17 seasons of his stellar playing career (1891–1907). In 1899, McGraw was the player-manager of the N.L.'s Baltimore Orioles. The team disbanded the next season when the N.L. contracted from 12 to eight teams, and McGraw was sold to the St. Louis Cardinals. His contract paid him $10,000, the highest total up to that time in baseball history, and included an exemption from baseball's reserve clause.

McGraw hit .344 for St. Louis in 1900, but that reserve-clause exclusion made it possible for him to leave the following season when the A.L. was formed and included a new team back in Baltimore. McGraw became part owner and manager of this 1901 edition of the Orioles. After a season of bickering with the A.L.'s President, Ban Johnson, McGraw jumped back to the N.L. to skipper the New York Giants to 10 pennants and three World Series titles between 1902 and 1932.

Library of Congress

Inducted into the Hall of Fame as a manager in 1937 by the Veterans Committee

Positions: *Shortstop, Third Base, Outfield, Manager*

Batted: *Left* **Threw:** *Right*

Height: *5' 7"* **Weight:** *155 lbs.*

Born: *April 7, 1873, in Truxton, NY*

Died: *February 25, 1934, in New Rochelle, NY*

Buried: *New Cathedral Cemetery in Baltimore, MD*

Debut: *August 26, 1891, with the Baltimore Orioles*

Final game: *June 18, 1907, with the New York Giants*

Postseason: *3× World Series Champion (1905, 1921, 1922), 7× N.L. Pennant (1904, 1911–1913, 1917, 1923, 1924)*

Awards & Recognition: *Managed in MLB's first All-Star Game in 1933*

Nicknames: *Mugsy, Little Napoleon*

Number worn in St. Louis: *Played prior to numbers being worn*

John McGraw – HOF Career Managerial Stats

YEAR(S)	SEASONS	TEAM	LEAGUE	WON	LOST	W-L%	TIES	GAMES	EJECTIONS	PENNANTS	CHAMPIONSHIPS
1899	1	BAL	NL	86	62	.581	4	152	5	0	0
1901 - 1902	2	BAL	AL	94	96	.495	3	193	8	0	0
1902 - 1932	31	NYG	NL	2583	1790	.591	51	4424	108	10	3
Career Totals	**33**			**2763**	**1948**	**.586**	**58**	**4769**	**121**	**10**	**3**

John McGraw – Career Playing Stats – WAR: 45.7, Slash Line: .334 / .466 / .410

YEAR(S)	SEASONS	TEAM	LEAGUE	G	AB	R	H	2B	3B	HR	RBI	SB	BB	SO	BA
1891	1	BAL	AA	131	115	17	31	3	5	0	14	4	12	17	.270
1892 - 1899	9	BAL	NL	717	3048	823	1032	91	50	10	378	365	630	106	.336
1900	**1**	**STL**	**NL**	**99**	**334**	**84**	**115**	**10**	**4**	**2**	**33**	**29**	**85**	**9**	**.344**
1901 - 1902	2	BAL	AL	93	295	85	99	17	11	1	31	29	78	12	.336
1902 - 1907	6	NYG	NL	60	132	15	32	0	0	0	6	9	31	11	.242
Career Totals	**17**			**1100**	**3924**	**1024**	**1309**	**121**	**70**	**13**	**462**	**436**	**836**	**155**	**.334**

Cy Young

Denton True Young was the given name of baseball's winningest pitcher. Fans know him as "Cy," short for "cyclone," due to the speed and movement of his pitches. In honor of his greatness, Major League Baseball has presented the Cy Young Award to baseball's best pitchers every season since the year following his death in 1955.

Young had been pitching for the N.L.'s Cleveland Spiders since 1890, when the team's owners, the Robison Brothers, also bought St. Louis's N.L. team in 1899. Hoping to improve their St. Louis investment, the owners changed the team's name from the Browns to the Perfectos and moved the best players from Cleveland (including Young) to the St. Louis roster. The move led the 1899 Spiders to become the worst team in MLB history (20 wins and 134 losses). Their "best of the best" did not become champions in St. Louis, rising only from 12th to fifth place finishes in the 1899 and 1900 seasons, when the owners adopted another new team name: the Cardinals.

At age 32 and in the 10th year of his 22-season career, Young posted a 26–16 record in 1899 and then a 20–18 record the next season to gain 46 of his record-setting 511 MLB wins in St. Louis. Those two seasons in St. Louis came in the middle of 14 consecutive seasons of 20 or more wins, including five seasons exceeding 30 wins.

Young left St. Louis for Boston's newly formed A.L. team in 1901 when the Robisons refused to match the Red Sox's salary offer of $3,500. They believed the 34-year-old Young was nearly washed up. He proved them wrong. He pitched eight more years in Beantown, winning an additional 192 games before adding 33 more wins elsewhere in his final three seasons and ending his career in 1911.

Inducted into the Hall of Fame as a player in 1937 by vote of the BBWAA

Position: *Pitcher*

Batted: *Right* **Threw:** *Right*

Height: *6' 2"* **Weight:** *210 lbs.*

Born: *March 29, 1867, in Gilmore, OH*

Died: *November 4, 1955, in Newcomerstown, OH*

Buried: *Pioli Cemetery in Peoli, OH*

Debut: *August 6, 1890, with the Cleveland Spiders*

Final game: *October 6, 1911, with the Boston Rustlers (N.L.)*

Postseason: *World Series Champion 1903*

Awards & Recognition: *Pitching Triple Crown 1901, 5× Wins Leader (1892, 1895, 1901–1903), 2× ERA Leader (1892, 1901), 2× Strikeout Leader (1896, 1901), Perfect Game (May 5, 1904), 3 No-Hitters (1897, 1904, 1908)*

Nickname: *Cyclone*

Number worn in St. Louis: *Played prior to numbers being worn*

Cy Young – HOF Career Pitching Stats – WAR: 163.6

YEAR	TEAM	LEAGUE	W	L	ERA	G	CG	SHO	SV	IP	H	HR	BB	SO
1890	CLV	NL	9	7	3.47	17	16	0	0	147.2	145	6	30	39
1891	CLV	NL	27	22	2.85	55	43	0	2	423.2	431	4	140	147
1892	CLV	NL	36	12	1.93	53	48	9	0	453	363	8	118	168
1893	CLV	NL	33	16	3.36	53	42	1	2	422.2	442	10	103	102
1894	CLV	NL	26	21	3.94	52	44	2	1	408.2	488	19	106	108
1895	CLV	NL	35	10	3.26	47	36	4	0	369.2	363	10	75	121
1896	CLV	NL	28	15	3.24	51	42	5	3	414.1	477	7	62	140
1897	CLV	NL	21	19	3.78	46	35	2	0	335.2	391	7	49	88
1898	CLV	NL	25	13	2.53	46	40	1	0	377.2	387	6	41	101
1899	**STL**	**NL**	**26**	**16**	**2.58**	**44**	**40**	**4**	**1**	**369.1**	**368**	**10**	**44**	**111**
1900	**STL**	**NL**	**20**	**18**	**3.00**	**41**	**32**	**4**	**0**	**321.1**	**337**	**7**	**36**	**115**
1901	BOS	AL	33	10	1.62	43	38	5	0	371.1	324	6	37	158
1902	BOS	AL	32	11	2.15	45	41	3	0	384.2	350	6	53	160
1903	BOS	AL	28	9	2.08	40	34	7	2	341.2	294	6	37	176
1904	BOS	AL	26	16	1.97	43	40	10	1	380	327	6	29	200
1905	BOS	AL	18	19	1.82	38	31	4	0	320.2	248	3	30	210
1906	BOS	AL	13	21	3.19	39	28	0	2	287.2	288	3	25	140
1907	BOS	AL	21	15	1.99	43	33	6	2	343.1	286	3	51	147
1908	BOS	AL	21	11	1.26	36	30	3	2	299	230	1	37	150
1909	CLV	AL	19	15	2.26	35	30	3	0	294.1	267	4	59	109
1910	CLV	AL	7	10	2.53	21	14	1	0	163.1	149	0	27	58
1911	CLV	AL	3	4	3.88	7	4	0	0	46.1	54	2	13	20
1911	BOS	NL	4	5	3.71	11	8	2	0	80	83	4	15	35
Career Totals			**511**	**315**	**2.63**	**906**	**749**	**76**	**18**	**7356**	**7092**	**138**	**1217**	**2803**
STL (2 yrs)			**46**	**34**	**2.78**	**85**	**72**	**8**	**1**	**690.2**	**705**	**17**	**80**	**236**

Wikimedia Commons

Grover Cleveland Alexander

Named after the sitting US President when he was born, Grover Cleveland Alexander would be played by the man who would become the 40th president (Ronald Reagan) in a 1952 Hollywood biopic. Despite the presidential aura of his name, Alexander preferred being called "Old Pete."

Alexander came to St. Louis as one of the game's best pitchers. His 1911 debut with the Philadelphia Phillies remains the game's greatest pitching season by a rookie. In his next six seasons he would post a 162–75 record while winning more than 30 games three times. The Phillies, fearing that Alexander would be drafted with America at war in 1917, traded him to the Cubs. Wounded in battle, Alexander returned home with shell shock and epilepsy, and developed alcoholism as he attempted to find relief from the trauma he suffered.

Despite these scars of war, Alexander came back to the Cubs in 1919 and remained a fixture with the team before being claimed off waivers by the Cardinals in June 1926. His drinking had become an issue in Chicago, but Cards skipper Rogers Hornsby tolerated it while Old Pete's 9–7 record helped the Redbirds win their first N.L. title, and Alexander's World Series heroics made him legendary.

After complete-game wins in Game Two and Game Six over the Yankees, Alexander thought his Series was over. Napping in the bullpen during Game Seven, he was brought in to hold a 3–2 lead with the bases loaded and two outs in the seventh inning. In a dramatic showdown, he struck out the dangerous Tony Lazzeri. Alexander then held the New Yorkers in check through the bottom of the ninth, when Babe Ruth was caught stealing second base for the final out of the game and Series. Alexander spent three more seasons with the Cardinals, helping the team to the 1928 World Series before pitching the final nine games of his career back in Philadelphia in 1930.

Wikimedia Commons

Inducted into the Hall of Fame as a player in 1938 by vote of the BBWAA

Position: *Pitcher*

Batted: *Right* **Threw:** *Right*

Height: *6′ 1″* **Weight:** *185 lbs.*

Born: *February 26, 1887, in Elba, NE*

Died: *November 4, 1950, in St. Paul, NE*

Buried: *Elmwood Cemetery in St. Paul, NE*

Debut: *April 15, 1911, with the Philadelphia Phillies*

Final game: *May 28, 1930, with the Philadelphia Phillies*

Postseason: *World Series Champion (1926) 3× N.L. Pennant (1915, 1926, 1928)*

Awards & Recognition: *3× Pitching Triple Crown (1915, 1916, 1920), 6× N.L. Wins Leader (1911, 1914–1917, 1920), 4× N.L. ERA Leader (1915, 1916, 1919, 1920), 6× N.L. Strikeout Leader (1912, 1914–1917)*

Nickname: *Old Pete*

Number worn in St. Louis: *Played prior to numbers being worn*

Grover Cleveland Alexander – HOF Pitching Stats – WAR: 119.6

YEAR	TM	LG	W	L	ERA	G	CG	SHO	SV	IP	H	HR	BB	SO
1911	PHI	NL	28	13	2.57	48	31	7	3	367.0	285	5	129	227
1912	PHI	NL	19	17	2.81	46	25	3	3	310.1	289	11	105	195
1913	PHI	NL	22	8	2.79	47	23	9	2	306.1	288	9	75	159
1914	PHI	NL	27	15	2.38	46	32	6	1	355.0	327	8	76	214
1915	PHI	NL	31	10	1.22	49	36	12	3	376.1	253	3	64	241
1916	PHI	NL	33	12	1.55	48	38	16	3	389.0	323	6	50	167
1917	PHI	NL	30	13	1.83	45	34	8	0	388.0	336	4	56	200
1918	CHC	NL	2	1	1.73	3	3	0	0	26.0	19	0	3	15
1919	CHC	NL	16	11	1.72	30	20	9	1	235.0	180	3	38	121
1920	CHC	NL	27	14	1.91	46	33	7	5	363.1	335	8	69	173
1921	CHC	NL	15	13	3.39	31	20	3	1	252.0	286	10	33	77
1922	CHC	NL	16	13	3.63	33	20	1	1	245.2	283	8	34	48
1923	CHC	NL	22	12	3.19	39	26	3	2	305.0	308	17	30	72
1924	CHC	NL	12	5	3.03	21	12	0	0	169.1	183	9	25	33
1925	CHC	NL	15	11	3.39	32	20	1	0	236.0	270	15	29	63
1926	TOT	NL	12	10	3.05	30	15	2	2	200.1	191	8	31	47
1926	CHC	NL	3	3	3.46	7	4	0	0	52.0	55	0	7	12
1926	**STL**	**NL**	**9**	**7**	**2.91**	**23**	**11**	**2**	**2**	**148.1**	**136**	**8**	**24**	**35**
1927	**STL**	**NL**	**21**	**10**	**2.52**	**37**	**22**	**2**	**3**	**268.0**	**261**	**11**	**38**	**48**
1928	**STL**	**NL**	**16**	**9**	**3.36**	**34**	**18**	**1**	**2**	**243.2**	**262**	**15**	**37**	**59**
1929	**STL**	**NL**	**9**	**8**	**3.89**	**22**	**8**	**0**	**0**	**132.0**	**149**	**10**	**23**	**33**
1930	PHI	NL	0	3	9.14	9	0	0	0	21.2	40	5	6	6
Career Totals			**373**	**208**	**2.56**	**696**	**436**	**90**	**32**	**5190.0**	**4868**	**165**	**951**	**2198**
STL (4 yrs)			**55**	**34**	**3.08**	**116**	**59**	**5**	**7**	**792.0**	**808**	**44**	**122**	**175**

Missouri Historical Society, St. Louis

Charles Comiskey

Charles Comiskey owned the Chicago White Sox and the South Side stadium that carried his name. His 50-plus-year baseball career began in St. Louis with the American Association's (A.A.) St. Louis Browns, a team he managed and played for between 1882 and 1889, and a return season in 1891. The Browns were league champions for four straight years between 1885 and 1888. In 1886 they became the only A.A. team ever to beat the N.L. champion in the annual postseason championship series played between the two leagues.

Comiskey spent the first eight years of his 13-year career with the St. Louis Browns as a player-manager playing first base. His Hall of Fame plaque notes that he was the "first man at his position to play away from the bag." Not a tremendous hitter in an era of higher averages, his career batting average was only .264 (.273 with St. Louis). He did have one standout season with the Browns in 1887, when he batted .335 while driving in 103 runs. His managing career was much better. As a manager for 12 seasons, Comiskey was 839–540 (562–272 in St. Louis).

Selected into the Hall of Fame's fourth class as a pioneer/executive, Comiskey became owner of the Western League's St. Paul Saints in 1895. He moved the team to Chicago in 1900 as the White Stockings and then navigated them into the newly formed A.L. in 1901 as the White Sox. His teams were quite successful, winning two A.L. pennants and two World Championships in the 20 seasons between 1901 and 1919. Unfortunately, under his tenure, one of baseball's darkest moments occurred with the "Black Sox" scandal, when several of his players conspired to throw the 1919 World Series to the Cincinnati Reds. Comiskey would own the Sox until his death in 1931.

Wikimedia Commons

Inducted into the Hall of Fame as a pioneer/executive in 1939 by the Old Timer's Committee

Positions: *First Base, Manager, Owner*

Batted: *Right* **Threw:** *Right*

Height: *6' 0"* **Weight:** *180 lbs.*

Born: *August 15, 1859, in Chicago, IL*

Died: *October 26, 1931, in Eagle River, WI*

Buried: *Calvary Catholic Cemetery in Evanston, IL*

Debut: *May 2, 1882, with the St. Louis Browns (N.L.)*

Final game: *September 12, 1894, with the Cincinnati Reds*

Postseason: *A.A. World Champion (1886), 4× A.A. Pennant (1885, 1886, 1887, 1889), 2× MLB World Series Champion (1906, 1917), 4× A.L. Pennant (1901, 1906, 1917, 1919)*

Nicknames: *Commy, the Old Roman*

Number worn in St. Louis: *Played prior to numbers being worn*

Charles Comiskey – HOF Executive Stats

YEAR(S)	SEASONS	TEAM	LEAGUE	WON	LOST	W-L%	TIES	GAMES	PENNANTS	CHAMPIONSHIPS
1901 - 1931	31	CHW	AL	2391	2260	.507	62	4651	4	2

Charles Comiskey – Career Managerial Stats

YEAR(S)	SEASONS	TEAM	LEAGUE	WON	LOST	W-L%	TIES	GAMES	EJECTIONS	PENNANTS	CHAMPIONSHIPS
1883 - 1889	7	STL	AA	477	221	.671	13	711	0	4	1
1890	1	CHW	PL	75	62	.547	1	138	0	0	0
1891	1	STL	AA	85	51	.625	3	139	0	0	0
1892 - 1894	3	CINN	NL	202	206	.495	12	420	2	0	0
Career Totals	12			839	540	.608	29	1408	2	4	1
Career	8	STL	AA	562	272	.674	16	850	0	4	1

Charles Comiskey – Career Playing Stats – WAR: 7.6, Slash Line: .264 / .293 / .337

YEAR(S)	SEASONS	TEAM	LEAGUE	G	AB	R	H	2B	3B	HR	RBI	SB	BB	SO	BA
1882 - 1889	8	STL	AA	895	3809	730	1046	145	56	23	601	295	102	67	.275
1890	1	CHI	PL	88	377	53	92	11	3	0	59	34	14	17	.244
1891	1	STL	AA	139	572	84	148	16	2	2	88	38	33	25	.259
1892 - 1894	3	CIN	NL	268	1038	125	243	35	7	3	135	49	48	23	.234
Career Totals	13			1390	5796	992	1529	207	68	28	883	416	197	132	.264
Career	9	STL	AA	1034	4381	814	1194	161	58	25	689	333	135	92	.273

Getty Images

Rogers Hornsby

Perhaps the greatest right-handed batter in MLB history, Hornsby was a seven-time NL batting champion. During six of those seven years (from 1920 to 1925), Hornsby averaged .402. Three times during that span he hit over. 400. His 23-season career batting average was an amazing .3585–fourth behind Josh Gibson's .3716, Ty Cobb's .3662, and Oscar Charleston's .3648. And Hornsby wasn't just about getting hits. Twice he led the N.L. in home runs, and he was the league RBI leader four times. Twice this offensive prowess led Hornsby to the Triple Crown along with two MVP selections.

Hornsby's big-league career began with the Cardinals in 1915. He played with the team through the 1926 season, taking over as manager in 1925 and leading the Redbirds to their first pennant and World Championship in 1926. His reward was a trade to the New York Giants for Frankie Frisch shortly after the Series. While there was never any doubt about Hornsby's baseball abilities, as an individual he was a complicated person. He never drank, smoked, or attended movie theaters (the biggest form of entertainment in his day) because he did not wish to strain his eyes. It was difficult for Hornsby to relate to people. He didn't understand why players could not compete at the level he did (few ever have), and he always thought he knew more than everyone else, a quality that often led to his wearing out his welcome despite his outstanding play. During the years 1926–1928 and 1930, Hornsby would manage four different teams (he didn't manage in 1929). Whether he mellowed or not, he would eventually manage two other teams and compile a 14-year total managing career. It wasn't his managing that got him to the Hall of Fame, though; it was his record-setting hitting skills. The stats speak for themselves. There was no better right-handed hitter in the history of baseball.

Wikimedia Commons

Inducted into the Hall of Fame as a player in 1942 by the BBWAA

Positions: *Second Base, Manager*

Batted: *Right* **Threw:** *Right*

Height: *5' 11"* **Weight:** *175 lbs.*

Born: *April 27, 1896, in Winters, TX*

Died: *January 5, 1963, in Chicago, IL*

Buried: *Hornsby Bend Cemetery, Hornsby Bend, TX*

Debut: *September 10, 1915, with the St. Louis Cardinals*

Final game: *July 20, 1937, with the St. Louis Browns*

Postseason: *1x World Series Champion (1926), 2x N.L. Pennant (1926, 1929)*

Awards & Recognition: *2× N.L. MVP (1925, 1929), 2× Triple Crown (1922, 1925), 7× N.L. Batting Champion (1920–1925, 1928), 2× N.L. Home Run Leader (1922, 1925), 4× N.L. RBI Leader (1920–1922, 1925)*

Nickname: *Rajah*

Number worn in St. Louis: *Cardinals (4, 6), Browns (16, 11, 4)*

Rogers Hornsby – Career Managerial Stats

YEAR(S)	SEASONS	TEAM	LEAGUE	WON	LOST	W-L%	TIES	GAMES	EJECTIONS	PENNANTS	CHAMPIONSHIPS
1925 - 1926	**2**	**STL**	**NL**	**153**	**116**	**.569**	**2**	**271**	**2**	**1**	**1**
1927	1	NYG	NL	22	10	.688	1	33	0	0	0
1928	1	BSN	NL	39	83	.320	0	122	1	0	0
1930 - 1932	3	CHC	NL	141	116	.549	2	259	1	0	0
1933 - 1937, 1952	**6**	**SLB**	**AL**	**255**	**381**	**.401**	**11**	**647**	**1**	**0**	**0**
1952 - 1953	2	CIN	NL	91	106	.462	1	198	0	0	0
Career Totals	14			701	812	.463	17	1530	5	1	1

Rogers Hornsby – HOF Career Playing Stats – WAR: 127.0, Slash Line: .258 / .434 / .577

YEAR(S)	SEASONS	TEAM	LEAGUE	G	AB	R	H	2B	3B	HR	RBI	SB	BB	SO	BA
1915 - 1926, 1933	**13**	**STL**	**NL**	**1580**	**5881**	**1089**	**2110**	**367**	**143**	**193**	**1072**	**118**	**660**	**480**	**.359**
1927	1	NYG	NL	155	568	133	205	32	9	26	125	9	86	38	.361
1928	1	BSN	NL	140	486	99	188	42	7	21	94	5	107	41	.387
1929 - 1932	4	CHC	NL	317	1121	245	392	91	10	58	264	3	165	104	.350
1933 - 1937	**5**	**SLB**	**AL**	**67**	**117**	**13**	**35**	**9**	**0**	**3**	**29**	**0**	**20**	**16**	**.299**
Career Totals	23			2259	8173	1579	2930	541	169	301	1584	135	1038	679	.358

Wikimedia Commons

Roger Bresnahan

Roger Bresnahan's Hall of Fame plaque calls him "one of the games most natural players" and states that he "might have starred at any position." He did, however, leave his mark on one position in particular: catcher. His mentor, John McGraw described him as one of the best catchers he had ever seen.

Bresnahan revolutionized the catching position. In 1907, he became the first catcher in MLB history to wear shin guards and later a padded facemask. On the other side of the plate, Bresnahan developed the first batting helmet after being hit on the head by a pitch. He began his career throwing pitches rather than catching them. In his MLB debut with the Washington Senators, Bresnahan threw a six-hit shutout against the St. Louis Browns.

Even though he went 4–0 in Washington, Bresnahan was released after his first season due to a salary dispute. He bounced around other leagues before catching the eye of manager John McGraw of the newly formed A.L. Baltimore Orioles in 1901. He became their backup catcher and part-time outfielder. When McGraw jumped to the (N.L.) Giants in 1902, Bresnahan joined the skipper at midseason. He became the Giants' primary catcher in 1905 when the Giants won the pennant. Bresnahan caught all five games of the ensuing Fall Classic, which included three shutouts by batterymate Christy Mathewson and a fourth by teammate Joe McGinnity.

After the 1908 season, the Cardinals traded their best hitter and pitcher to get Bresnahan as their player–manager. He spent four seasons at their helm and only once did his team finish as high as fifth place. As the hoped-for success was never realized, Bresnahan fell into disfavor with Redbird ownership, was fired as manager, and was sold to the Chicago Cubs. He would play with the Cubs for three more years before becoming their player–manager in his final season in 1915.

Library of Congress

Inducted into the Hall of Fame as a player in 1945 by the Old Timers Committee

Positions: *Pitcher, Catcher, Outfielder, Manager*

Batted: *Right* **Threw:** *Right*

Height: *5' 9"* **Weight:** *200 lbs.*

Born: *June 11, 1879, in Toledo, OH*

Died: *December 4, 1944, in Toledo, OH*

Buried: *Calvary Cemetery, Toledo OH*

Debut: *August 27, 1897, with the Washington Senators*

Final game: *October 3, 1915, with the Chicago Cubs*

Postseason: *World Series Champion (1905), N.L. Pennant (1905)*

Nickname: *The Duke of Tralee*

Number worn in St. Louis: *Played prior to numbers being worn*

Roger Bresnahan – Career Managerial Stats

YEAR(S)	SEASONS	TEAM	LEAGUE	WON	LOST	W-L%	TIES	GAMES	EJECTIONS	PENNANTS	CHAMPIONSHIPS
1909	1	STL	NL	54	98	.355	2	154	10	0	0
1910	1	STL	NL	63	90	.412	0	153	4	0	0
1911	1	STL	NL	75	74	.503	9	158	4	0	0
1912	1	STL	NL	63	90	.412	0	153	5	0	0
1915	1	CHC	NL	73	80	.477	3	156	6	0	0
Career Totals	5			328	432	.432	14	774	29	0	0
1909-1912	4	STL	NL	255	352	.420	11	618	23	0	0

Roger Bresnahan – HOF Career Playing Stats – WAR: 42.9, Slash Line: .279 / .386 / .377

YEAR(S)	SEASONS	TEAM	LEAGUE	G	AB	R	H	2B	3B	HR	RBI	SB	BB	SO	BA
1897	1	WHS	NL	6	16	1	6	0	0	0	3	0	1	2	.375
1900, 1913 - 1915	4	CHC	NL	249	633	81	151	23	7	2	64	40	99	54	.239
1901 - 1902	2	BLA	AL	151	530	70	143	17	15	5	66	22	44	49	.270
1902 - 1908	7	NYG	NL	751	2499	438	731	135	35	15	291	118	410	234	.293
1908 - 1912	4	STL	NL	289	803	92	221	43	14	4	106	32	160	64	.275
Career Totals	17			1446	4481	682	1252	218	71	26	530.0	212	714	403	.279

Library of Congress

Wilbert Robinson

Wilbert Robinson went by the nickname "Uncle Robbie" during baseball's early years. In his 36-season career, Robinson only spent one year as a player in St. Louis. It was a career in which he left a special mark on the game as a player, coach, and then manager. As with so many of these early inductees, Robinson's career began in the A.A. He caught on as a catcher with the Philadelphia Athletics, later spending time with the Baltimore Orioles before their move to the N.L. in 1892. In Baltimore Robinson played on three straight N.L. pennant winning teams (1894–1896). When the N.L. shifted from 12 teams to eight in 1900, the Baltimore team was no longer. Robinson was sold, along with John McGraw, to the St. Louis Cardinals. Both players played just one season in St. Louis before jumping back to Baltimore's entry in the newly formed A.L. in 1901. McGraw served as the Orioles' first player–manager but left for the New York Giants after just a year and a half, leaving Robinson to finish the 1902 season as Baltimore's player–manager. It was an instrumental move that turned a career .273 hitting catcher into a Hall of Fame manager.

Yet the rise to managerial stardom was not immediate. Robinson left the game before joining McGraw's Giants for a three-year stint as a coach in 1911. Despite the Giants winning three straight pennants, a dispute between McGraw and Robison arose after the 1913 season that sent the latter heading south to the borough of Brooklyn, where Uncle Robbie would begin an 18-year tenure as manager of the Dodgers. After delivering their first ever pennant in 1916, the team even adopted the "Robins" moniker in recognition of their new manager. Robinson would bring another pennant to Brooklyn in 1920 before turning over the helm of the team in 1931.

Library of Congress

Inducted into the Hall of Fame as a manager in 1945 by the Old-Timers Committee

Positions: *Catcher, Manager*

Batted: *Right* **Threw:** *Right*

Height: *5' 8"* **Weight:** *215 lbs.*

Born: *June 29, 1864, in Bolton, MA*

Died: *August 8, 1934, in Atlanta, GA*

Buried: *New Cathedral Cemetery in Baltimore, MD*

Debut: *April 18, 1886, with the Philadelphia Athletics*

Final game: *September 29, 1902, with the Baltimore Orioles*

Postseason: *5× N.L. Pennant (Player: 1894–1896, Manager: 1916, 1920)*

Awards & Recognition: *Recorded seven hits in seven at bats on June 10, 1892*

Nickname: *Uncle Robbie*

Number worn in St. Louis: *Played prior to numbers being worn*

Wilbert Robinson – HOF Career Managerial Stats

YEAR(S)	SEASONS	TEAM	LEAGUE	WON	LOST	W-L%	TIES	GAMES	EJECTIONS	PENNANTS	CHAMPIONSHIPS
1902	1	BLA	AL	24	57	.296	2	83	0	0	0
1914 - 1931	18	BRO	NL	1375	1341	.506	19	2735	3	2	0
Career Totals	**19**			**1399**	**1398**	**.500**	**21**	**2818**	**3**	**2**	**0**

Wilbert Robinson – Career Playing Stats – WAR: 6.7, Slash Line: .273 / .316 / .346

YEAR(S)	SEASONS	TEAM	LEAGUE	G	AB	R	H	2B	3B	HR	RBI	SB	BB	SO	BA
1886 - 1890	5	PHA	AA	372	1453	180	330	50	13	7	155	88	66	75	.227
1890 - 1891	2	BAL	AA	107	382	32	85	9	5	2	50	19	19	37	.223
1892 - 1899	8	BLN	NL	673	2456	329	751	120	22	8	406	62	168	158	.306
1900	**1**	**STL**	**NL**	**60**	**210**	**26**	**52**	**5**	**1**	**0**	**28**	**7**	**11**	**20**	**.248**
1901 - 1902	2	BLA	AL	159	574	70	170	28	10	1	83	20	22	33	.296
Career Totals	**17**			**1371**	**5075**	**637**	**1388**	**212**	**51**	**18**	**722**	**196**	**286**	**323**	**.273**

Wikimedia Commons

Jesse Burkett

Jesse Burkett was one of baseball's best hitters throughout its early years. During his 16-year career (1890–1905), Burkett twice hit better than .400 while topping the N.L. batting charts three times. Prior to 1902 MLB rules did not count foul balls as strikes, and Burkett was noted as one of the game's best at fouling off pitches. With fouls not impacting his count at the plate, he would continue to foul off pitches until he got the one he wanted and then drove it for a hit. Standing only 5' 8" he didn't have what's called "home-run power," but Burkett did set home-run records—with inside-the-park home runs. Burkett still holds the record for the most inside-the-park home runs in MLB history (55).

But it wasn't his prowess with the bat that got Jesse to the majors. He joined the 1890 Giants as a pitcher whose first season mark (3–10) didn't offer much promise. However, he also played center field, and his .309 hitting earned him a spot on the team. After that rookie season in New York, his next eight were in Cleveland with Frank Robison's Spiders, and he twice hit over .400. In 1899 Burkett was transferred along with Cy Young to Robison's other team, the St. Louis Perfectos, where Burkett thought he hit .400. Burkett's Hall of Fame plaque gives him credit for attaining the .400 mark three times. Later research adjusted his average for the 1899 season down to .396. In 1901 he won his third and final batting crown with a .376 average. At season's end, he jumped to the city's new A.L. Browns, where he would play another three years before his final season with the A.L.'s Boston Americans in 1905. Burkett left his mark on baseball beyond his home-run record. For 15 years he held the MLB single-season hits record and today still has the highest batting average (.378) and on-base percentage (.444) in Cardinals history.

Wikimedia Commons

Inducted into the Hall of Fame as a player in 1946 by the Old Timers Committee

Positions: *Pitcher, Outfield*

Batted: *Left* **Threw:** *Left*

Height: *5' 8"* **Weight:** *155 lbs.*

Born: *December 4, 1868, in Wheeling, WV*

Died: *May 27, 1953, in Worcester, MA*

Buried: *St. John Cemetery, Worcester MA*

Debut: *April 22, 1890, with the New York Giants*

Final game: *October 7, 1905, with the Boston Americans*

Postseason: *N.L. Pennant 1892*

Awards & Recognition: *3× N.L. Batting Champion (1895, 1896, 1901)*

Nickname: *Crab*

Number worn in St. Louis: *Played prior to numbers being worn*

Jesse Burkett – HOF Playing Stats – WAR: 59.7 / .338 / .415 / .446

SEASON	TEAM	LG	G	AB	R	H	2B	3B	HR	RBI	SB	BB	SO	BA
1890	NYG	NL	101	401	67	124	23	13	4	60	14	33	52	.309
1891	CLV	NL	40	167	29	45	7	4	0	13	1	23	19	.269
1892	CLV	NL	145	608	119	167	15	14	6	66	36	67	59	.275
1893	CLV	NL	125	511	145	178	25	15	6	82	39	98	23	.348
1894	CLV	NL	125	523	138	187	27	14	8	94	28	84	27	.358
1895	CLV	NL	132	555	153	225	22	13	5	83	41	74	32	.405
1896	CLV	NL	133	586	160	240	27	16	6	72	34	49	19	.410
1897	CLV	NL	127	517	129	198	28	7	2	60	28	76	25	.383
1898	CLV	NL	150	624	114	213	18	9	0	42	19	69	30	.341
1899	**STL**	**NL**	**141**	**558**	**116**	**221**	**21**	**8**	**7**	**71**	**25**	**67**	**23**	**.396**
1900	**STL**	**NL**	**141**	**559**	**88**	**203**	**11**	**15**	**7**	**68**	**32**	**62**	**35**	**.363**
1901	**STL**	**NL**	**142**	**601**	**142**	**226**	**20**	**15**	**10**	**75**	**27**	**59**	**70**	**.376**
1902	**SLB**	**AL**	**138**	**553**	**97**	**169**	**29**	**9**	**5**	**52**	**23**	**71**	**25**	**.306**
1903	**SLB**	**AL**	**132**	**515**	**73**	**151**	**20**	**7**	**3**	**40**	**17**	**52**	**47**	**.293**
1904	**SLB**	**AL**	**147**	**575**	**72**	**156**	**15**	**10**	**2**	**27**	**12**	**78**	**64**	**.271**
1905	BOS	AL	148	573	78	147	12	13	4	47	13	67	63	.257
Career Totals			**2067**	**8426**	**1720**	**2850**	**320**	**182**	**75**	**952**	**389**	**1029**	**613**	**.338**
STL (3 Yrs)		**NL**	**424**	**1718**	**346**	**650**	**52**	**38**	**24**	**214**	**84**	**188**	**128**	**.378**
SLB (3 Yrs)		**AL**	**417**	**1643**	**242**	**476**	**64**	**26**	**10**	**119**	**52**	**201**	**136**	**.290**

St. L

Clark Griffith

Before rising to fame as one of baseball's most recognized managers and owners, Clark Griffith began his 20-year pitching career (1891–1914, including four years in which he did not play) with the A.A.'s St. Louis Browns and not a full season at that. The toil of an 11–8 record through his first 27 games left Griffith with a sore arm. He was released and picked up by the Boston Reds and went 3–1 in seven more games of that rookie season. After the season, the A.A. folded. Griffith then bounced around in lesser leagues before joining the N.L.'s Chicago Colts (later renamed the Cubs) in September of 1893, and he posted a 152–96 record there over eight seasons.

When the A.L. was formed in 1901, Griffith jumped leagues and became player-manager of Chicago's new southside White Sox. His 24 wins led the Sox to the A.L.'s inaugural pennant. But it wasn't his 237 career wins that paved Griffith's way into the Hall of Fame. It was his work off the field that helped ensure that the A.L. would succeed. In 1903, when the Baltimore Orioles were moved to New York as the Highlanders (later renamed the Yankees). Griffith was appointed their first manager to help them succeed in the nation's biggest city. He stayed through the 1908 season before skippering the Cincinnati Reds for three seasons and then joining the Washington Nationals (aka Senators) as their manager and minority owner in 1912. Griffith would spend the next nine years as Washington's manager. After becoming the team's majority owner in 1919 he left the dugout for good after the 1920 season to focus on running his team for the next 36 seasons until his death in 1955. Clark Griffith served baseball well and remains the only man in MLB history to have been a professional player, manager, and owner for at least 20 years apiece.

Inducted into the Hall of Fame as a pioneer/ executive in 1946 by the Old Timers Committee

Positions: *Pitcher, Outfielder, Manager, Owner*

Batted: *Right* **Threw:** *Right*

Height: *5' 6"* **Weight:** *156 lbs.*

Born: *November 20, 1869, in Clear Creek, MO*

Died: *October 27, 1955, in Washington, D.C.*

Buried: *Fort Lincoln Cemetery, Brentwood, MD*

Debut: *April 11, 1891, with the St. Louis Browns (N.L.)*

Final game: *October 7, 1914, with the Washington Senators*

Postseason: *1× World Series Champion (1924—Owner), 4× A.L. Pennant (1901*—Player / Manager, 1924, 1925, 1933—Owner) *No Post-Season Championship Series*

Awards & Recognition: *MLB ERA Leader (1898)*

Nickname: *The Old Fox*

Number worn in St. Louis: *Played prior to numbers being worn*

Clark Griffith - HOF Career Owner / Executive Stats

YEAR(S)	SEASONS	TEAM	LEAGUE	WON	LOST	W-L%	TIES	GAMES	PENNANTS	CHAMPIONSHIPS
1920 - 1955	36	WSH	AL	2677	2835	.482	39	5551	3	1

Clark Griffith – Career Managerial Stats

YEAR(S)	SEASONS	TEAM	LEAGUE	WON	LOST	W-L%	TIES	GAMES	EJECTIONS	PENNANTS	CHAMPIONSHIPS
1901 - 1902	2	CHW	AL	157	113	.581	5	275	0	1	0
1903 - 1908	6	NYY	AL	419	370	.531	18	807	0	0	0
1909 - 1911	3	CIN	NL	222	238	.483	12	472	0	0	0
1912 - 1920	9	WSH	AL	693	646	.518	24	1363	0	0	0
Career Totals	**20**			**1491**	**1367**	**.522**	**59**	**2917**	**0**	**1**	**0**

Clark Griffith – Career Playing Stats – WAR: 63.8

YEAR(S)	SEASONS	TEAM	LEAGUE	W	L	ERA	G	CG	SHO	SV	IP	H	HR	BB	SO
1891	**1**	**STL**	**AA**	**11**	**8**	**3.33**	**27**	**12**	**0**	**2**	**186.1**	**195**	**8**	**58**	**68**
1891	1	BOS	AA	3	1	5.63	7	3	0	0	40	47	3	15	20
1893 - 1900	8	CHC	NL	152	96	3.40	265	240	9	1	2188.2	2445	42	517	573
1901 - 1902	2	CHW	AL	39	16	3.34	63	46	8	1	479.2	522	15	97	118
1903 - 1907	5	NYY	AL	32	24	2.66	87	35	5	3	483	447	7	85	172
1909	1	CIN	NL	0	1	6.00	1	1	0	0	6	11	0	2	3
1912 - 1914	3	WSH	AL	0	0	4.50	3	0	0	1	2	3	1	0	1
Career Totals	**20**			**237**	**146**	**3.31**	**453**	**337**	**22**	**8**	**3385**	**3670**	**76**	**774**	**955**

Library of Congress

Tommy McCarthy

Thomas Francis Michael McCarthy, the son of Irish immigrants, made a name for himself in baseball. Despite his ties to St. Louis baseball, his is a name most fans are not familiar with. Sandwiched between stints in the N.L., McCarthy spent four of his 13 seasons (1884–1896) playing on a very good St. Louis Browns A.A. team. He joined the club in their last year of a four-year run of league championships (1888). In his next three years the Browns would finish twice in second place along with a third-place finish before the League folded at the end of the 1891 season. McCarthy managed the Browns for the first 27 games of the 1890 season before falling out of favor with owner Chris Von der Ahe.

His induction into the Hall of Fame by the Veterans Committee led critics to question the standards and expectations for induction. While the outfielder's offensive numbers are not in the range of the great hitters of his era, McCarthy could be described as a productive hitter who became one of the game's earliest base-stealing artists, leading the N.L. in steals in 1890. While he had a decent career in St. Louis, McCarthy is better known for his time with the N.L.'s Boston Beaneaters (precursor of the Braves), where he teamed up with future Hall of Famer Hugh Duffy to form the "Heavenly Twins" of the 1892–1895 outfield that led Boston to pennants in 1892 and 1893. It was also while playing in Boston that McCarthy was given credit for bringing the hit-and-run play into the game of baseball. As a good defender in the field, McCarthy was also recognized as an innovator of using the outfield trap to trick opposing base runners into a fateful run between bases only to be thrown out.

Getty Images

Inducted into the Hall of Fame as a player in 1946 by the Old Timers Committee

Positions: *Outfield, Manager*

Batted: *Right* **Threw:** *Right*

Height: *5' 7"* **Weight:** *170 lbs.*

Born: *July 24, 1863, in Boston, MA*

Died: *August 5, 1922, in Boston MA*

Buried: *Mount Calvary Cemetery, Roslindale, MA*

Debut: *July 19, 1884, with the Boston Reds of the Union Association*

Final game: *September 26, 1896, with the Brooklyn Bridegrooms*

Postseason: *American Association Pennant (1888), World Series Champion (1892), N.L. Pennant (1892)*

Number worn in St. Louis: *Played prior to numbers being worn*

Tommy McCarthy – Career Managerial Stats

YEAR(S)	SEASONS	TEAM	LEAGUE	WON	LOST	W-L%	TIES	GAMES	EJECTIONS	PENNANTS	CHAMPIONSHIPS
1890	1	STL	AA	15	12	.556	0	27	0	0	0
Career Totals	1			15	12	.556	0	27	0	0	0

Tommy McCarthy – HOF Playing Stats – WAR: 14.6, Slash Line: .292 / .364 / .375

SEASON	TEAM	LG	G	AB	R	H	2B	3B	HR	RBI	SB	BB	SO	BA
1884	BOS	UA	53	209	37	45	2	2	0			6		.215
1885	BSN	NL	40	148	16	27	2	0	0	11		5	25	.182
1886	PHI	NL	8	27	6	5	2	1	0	3	1	2	3	.185
1887	PHI	NL	18	70	7	13	4	0	0	6	15	2	5	.186
1888	STL	AA	131	511	107	140	20	3	1	68	93	38	22	.274
1889	STL	AA	140	604	136	176	24	7	2	63	57	46	26	.291
1890	STL	AA	133	548	137	192	28	9	6	69	83	66		.350
1891	STL	AA	134	570	124	176	20	6	8	92	37	49	19	.309
1892	BSN	NL	152	603	119	146	19	5	4	63	53	93	29	.242
1893	BSN	NL	116	462	107	160	28	6	5	111	46	64	10	.346
1894	BSN	NL	127	539	118	188	21	8	13	126	43	59	17	.349
1895	BSN	NL	117	452	90	131	13	2	2	73	18	72	12	.290
1896	BRO	NL	104	377	62	94	8	4	3	47	22	34	17	.249
Career Totals			1273	5120	1066	1493	191	53	44	732	468	536	185	.292
STL (4 Yrs)		AA	538	2233	504	684	92	25	17	292	270	199	67	.306

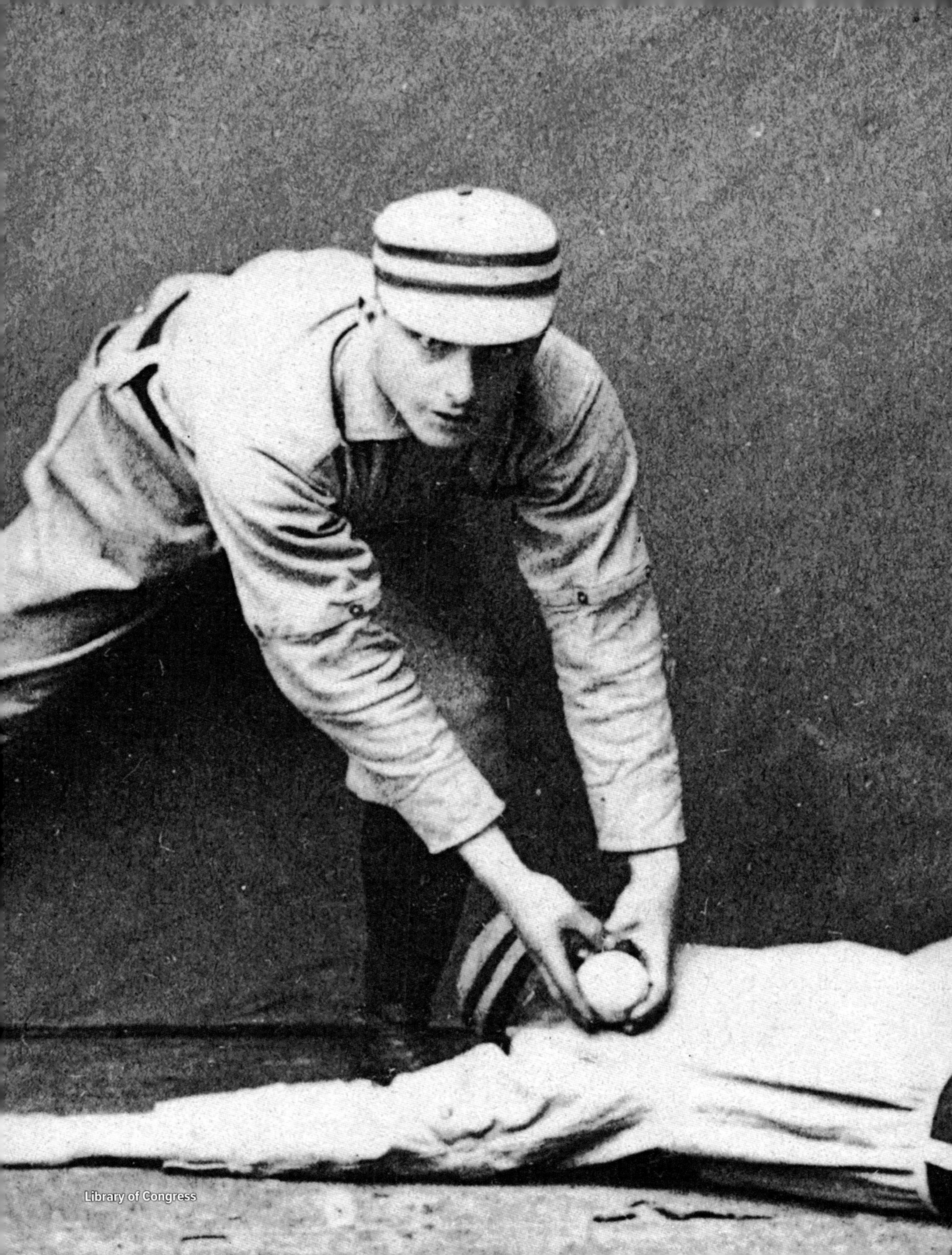

Frankie Frisch

On the field Frankie Frisch was one of baseball's best. He had it all: good speed, good glove, and good bat. More importantly, he was a winner. Eight times in his 19-year playing career Frisch was on a pennant-winning team, and he won four World Championships. But that was just his time as a player. He spent 16 seasons managing, and he was the player–manager of the World Champion Cardinals in 1934. He played for the Cardinals from 1927 to 1937—11 seasons in all, including five as their player–manager.

In college, Frisch was a multisport star at Fordham University in New York when his baseball skills caught the eye of Giants manager John McGraw. Christened with the nickname, "the Fordham Flash," Frisch left the university and went straight into the Giants lineup—never playing a single game in the minor leagues. In New York, Frisch sparkled, hitting .321 and stealing 224 bases during an eight-year tenure that included four pennants and two World Championships. In a common storyline, McGraw once more soured on one of his players. This time it was Frisch, who after the 1926 season was sent to the Cardinals in a trade for Rogers Hornsby.

Frisch flourished as a Redbird. Three times he would be an All-Star while also appearing in four World Series (1928, 1930, 1931, and 1934), winning two Championships (1931 and 1934). It was in that latter Championship season that Frisch served as player–manager of the "Gashouse Gang." He won the N.L. MVP in 1931 and led the league in steals three times during his career. His accomplishments made him one of the greatest players in the game and one of the best in Cardinals history.

Inducted into the Hall of Fame as a player in 1947 by the BBWAA

Position: *Second Base*

Batted: *Both* **Threw:** *Right*

Height: *5' 11"* **Weight:** *165 lbs.*

Born: *September 9, 1897, in Bronx, NY*

Died: *March 12, 1973, in Wilmington, DE*

Buried: *Woodlawn Cemetery, Bronx, NY*

Debut: *June 17, 1919, with the New York Giants*

Final game: *August 5, 1937, with the St. Louis Cardinals*

Postseason: *4× World Series Champion (1921, 1922, 1931, 1934), 8× N.L. Pennant (1921–1924, 1928, 1930–1931, 1934)*

Awards & Recognition: *3× All-Star (1933–1935), N.L. MVP (1931), 3× N.L. Stolen Base Leader (1921, 1927, 1931)*

Nickname: *The Fordham Flash*

Number worn in St. Louis: *Cardinals (3)*

Frankie Frisch – Career Managerial Stats

YEAR(S)	SEASONS	TEAM	LEAGUE	WON	LOST	W-L%	TIES	GAMES	EJECTIONS	PENNANTS	CHAMPIONSHIPS
1933 - 1938	**6**	**STL**	**NL**	**458**	**354**	**.564**	**10**	**822**	**21**	**1**	**1**
1940 - 1946	7	PIT	NL	539	528	.505	18	1085	51	0	0
1949 - 1951	3	CHC	NL	141	196	.418	2	339	16	0	0
Career Totals	**16**			**1138**	**1078**	**.514**	**30**	**2246**	**88**	**1**	**1**

Frankie Frisch – HOF Career Playing Stats – WAR: 71.8, Slash Line: .316 / .369 / .432

YEAR(S)	SEASONS	TEAM	LEAGUE	G	AB	R	H	2B	3B	HR	RBI	SB	BB	SO	BA
1919 - 1926	8	NYG	NL	1000	4053	701	1303	180	77	54	524	224	280	139	.321
1927 - 1937	**11**	**STL**	**NL**	**1311**	**5059**	**831**	**1577**	**286**	**61**	**51**	**720**	**195**	**448**	**133**	**.312**
Career Totals	**19**			**2311**	**9112**	**1532**	**2880**	**466**	**138**	**105**	**1244**	**419**	**728**	**272**	**.316**

Getty Images

Mordecai Brown

Mordecai Brown was nicknamed "Three Finger Brown" due to two different farm-equipment injuries he suffered as a child that cost him parts of two fingers on his right hand. The injuries eventually worked to his advantage by forcing him to adjust his grip on the ball. The unorthodox grip gave a unique downward movement to his curveball, the pitch that would lead him to the Hall of Fame.

It was also the pitch that brought Brown to St. Louis in 1903 to begin a 14-year career that included 12 years in the majors and two in the "renegade" Federal League. His lone season with the Cardinals did not get off to a Hall of Fame start. While his rookie ERA was a solid 2.60, his 9–13 record was indicative of the team's last place finish 46½ games out of first.

While looking for help out of the cellar after that season, the Cardinals made one of the worst trades in their history. They packaged Brown to the Cubs, where he became the pitcher Chicago needed to become a great team. In his first nine seasons in Chicago Brown won 186 games. More importantly, he helped lead the team to two World Championships in their four pennant-winning years between 1906 and 1910.

Health issues led to Brown's release after the 1912 season. After a year with the Reds in Cincinnati, Brown went back to St. Louis in 1914, but not with the Cardinals. He became the player–manager of the St. Louis Terriers of the new rival Federal League. He was released late in the season and hung on elsewhere in the Federal League for another season before ending his career back in Chicago with the Cubs. Brown went out in style with a game for the ages, losing to his nemesis Christy Mathewson in the final game that each of the two legends would pitch.

Wikimedia Commons

Inducted into the Hall of Fame as a player in 1949 by the Old Timers Committee

Positions: *Pitcher, Manager*

Batted: *Both* **Threw:** *Right*

Height: *5' 10"* **Weight:** *175 lbs.*

Born: *October 19, 1876, in Nyesville, IN*

Died: *February 14, 1948, in Terre Haute, IN*

Buried: *Roselawn Memorial Park, Terre Haute, IN*

Debut: *April 19, 1903, with the St. Louis Cardinals*

Final game: *September 4, 1916, with the Chicago Cubs*

Postseason: *2× World Series Champion (1907, 1908) 4× N.L. Pennant (1906–1908, 1910)*

Awards & Recognition: *N.L. Wins Leader (1909), MLB ERA Leader (1906)*

Nickname: *Three Finger*

Number worn in St. Louis: *Played prior to numbers being worn*

Mordecai Brown – Career Managerial Stats

YEAR(S)	SEASONS	TEAM	LEAGUE	WON	LOST	W-L%	TIES	GAMES	EJECTIONS	PENNANTS	CHAMPIONSHIPS
1914	1	SLM	FL	50	63	.442	1	114	1	0	0
Career Totals	1			50	63	.442	1	114	1	0	0

Mordecai Brown – HOF Career Playing Stats – WAR: 58.2

YEAR(S)	SEASONS	TEAM	LEAGUE	W	L	ERA	G	CG	SHO	SV	IP	H	HR	BB	SO
1903	1	STL	NL	9	13	2.6	26	19	1	0	201	231	7	59	83
1904 - 1912, 1916	10	CHC	NL	188	86	1.8	346	206	48	39	2329	1879	19	445	1043
1913	1	CIN	NL	11	12	2.91	39	11	1	6	173.1	174	7	44	41
1914	1	SLM	FL	12	6	3.29	26	13	2	0	175	172	7	43	81
1914	1	BIT	FL	2	5	4.21	9	5	0	0	57.2	63	1	18	32
1915	1	CHI	FL	17	8	2.09	35	17	3	4	236.1	189	2	64	95
Career Totals	14			239	130	2.06	481	271	55	49	3172	2708	43	673	1375

Wikimedia Commons

Kid Nichols

Charles "Kid" Nichols was one of baseball's best pitchers in the game's early years. Over a 15-year career spent entirely in the N.L., the righthanded pitcher went 362–208. For three straight seasons beginning in 1896, Nichols led the league in wins. Seven times he won more than 30 games in a season, a record that surely will never be broken in today's game.

Nichols's career began in Boston pitching for the Beaneaters (later renamed Braves) in 1890. During an eight-year span between 1891 and 1898, Nichols's pitching helped the team win five pennants. After a successful 1901 season in Boston, Nichols's career took a different path. He bought an interest in the Kansas City Blue Stockings Minor League Club and became the team's pitcher and manager. While his Kansas City team would cease operation late in the 1903 season due to financial constraints, the minor league stint set him up for his return to the majors the following season.

Nichols joined the previous year's last-place St. Louis Cardinals in 1904 as their manager with the expectation he would be pitching as well. Perhaps it was the managing skills Nichols learned in Kansas City, but it was more likely his 21–13 pitching record that helped move the team up three notches in the standings that year. Unfortunately, the following year was a different story, as personality issues with the Cardinals' owner led to his dismissal as manager in May. Nichols stayed on as a pitcher, but when the wins didn't come he was released in July. He caught on with the Phillies and played well enough to be signed for one more season in 1905, but injuries ended that season for Nichols, closing out the career of a youthful and slim pitcher who was given the nickname "Kid."

Inducted into the Hall of Fame as a player in 1949 by the Old Timers Committee

Positions: *Pitcher, Manager*

Batted: *Both* **Threw:** *Right*

Height: *5' 10"* **Weight:** *175 lbs.*

Born: *September 14, 1869, in Madison, WI*

Died: *April 11, 1953, in Kansas City, MO*

Buried: *Mount Moriah Cemetery in Kansas City, MO*

Debut: *April 23, 1890, with the Boston Beaneaters*

Final game: *May 18, 1906, with the Philadelphia Phillies*

Postseason: *5× N.L. Pennants (1891–1893, 1897, 1898)*

Awards & Recognition: *3× N.L. Wins Leader (1896–1898)*

Number worn in St. Louis: *Played prior to numbers being worn*

Kid Nichols – Career Managerial Stats

YEAR(S)	SEASONS	TEAM	LEAGUE	WON	LOST	W-L%	TIES	GAMES	EJECTIONS	PENNANTS	CHAMPIONSHIPS
1904	1	STL	NL	75	79	.487	1	155	0	0	0
1905	1	STL	NL	5	9	.357	0	14	0	0	0
Career Totals	2			80	88	.476	1	169	0	0	0

Kid Nichols – HOF Pitching Stats – WAR: 116.3

YEAR	TM	LG	W	L	ERA	G	CG	SHO	SV	IP	H	HR	BB	SO
1890	BSN	NL	27	19	2.23	48	47	7	0	424	374	8	112	222
1891	BSN	NL	30	17	2.39	52	45	5	3	425.1	413	15	103	240
1892	BSN	NL	35	16	2.84	53	49	5	0	453	404	15	121	192
1893	BSN	NL	34	14	3.52	52	43	1	1	425	426	15	118	94
1894	BSN	NL	32	13	4.75	50	40	3	0	407	488	23	121	113
1895	BSN	NL	27	16	3.41	48	43	1	2	390.2	434	15	90	148
1896	BSN	NL	30	14	2.83	49	37	3	1	372.1	387	14	101	102
1897	BSN	NL	31	11	2.64	46	37	2	3	368	362	9	68	127
1898	BSN	NL	31	12	2.13	50	40	5	4	388	316	7	85	138
1899	BSN	NL	21	19	2.99	42	37	4	1	343.1	326	11	82	108
1900	BSN	NL	13	16	3.07	29	25	4	0	231.1	215	11	72	53
1901	BSN	NL	19	16	3.22	38	33	4	0	321	306	8	90	143
1904	STL	NL	21	13	2.02	36	35	3	1	317	268	3	50	134
1905	STL	NL	1	5	5.40	7	5	0	0	51.2	64	1	18	16
1905	PHI	NL	10	6	2.27	17	15	1	0	138.2	129	1	28	50
1906	PHI	NL	0	1	9.82	4	1	0	0	11	17	0	13	1
Career Totals			362	208	2.96	621	532	48	16	5067.1	4929	156	1272	1881
STL (2 yrs)		NL	22	18	2.49	43	40	3	1	368.2	332	4	68	150

Wikimedia Commons

Dizzy Dean

Dizzy Dean was the "over-the-top" unofficial leader of the St. Louis Cardinals' "Gashouse Gang." The moniker "Dizzy" aptly reflected his actions both on and off the field. Had it not been for single appearances in his last two MLB seasons, Dizzy Dean would have joined Sandy Koufax as Hall of Famers who left the game at age 30.

In his first major league game, Dean tossed a three-hitter in the last game of the 1930 season. He stayed in the minors the next season but was back with the Cardinals in 1932. He led the N.L. in innings pitched in three of the next five seasons while twice leading the majors. He averaged 25 wins a year in his first five seasons. Dean's 1934 MVP season was the zenith of his career. Behind Dizzy's 30 wins and brother Paul's 19, the Cardinals won the N.L. pennant and beat the Detroit Tigers in the World Series. Each brother recorded two of the Cardinals' four wins in the Series. Dizzy's success continued for the next two seasons before fate and his stubbornness changed his career.

Struck on the toe by a line shot in the 1937 All-Star game, Dean refused to take the necessary time off to let the fracture heal. Instead, Dizzy changed his motion to avoid the pain while continuing to pitch. He wound up hurting his arm and his effectiveness. Traded to the Cubs the next season, Dizzy posted a 7-1 record in limited use, helping the Cubs win the 1938 pennant. He pushed his ailing arm through two more limited-use seasons before calling it quits in 1940 to bask in the national spotlight of the broadcast booth for the next 25 years.

But Dean's career wasn't quite finished. While broadcasting for the Browns in 1947, Dizzy became overly frustrated with the team's poor pitching to the point of declaring, "Doggone it, I can pitch better than nine out of the ten guys on this staff!" In typical Dizzy fashion he signed a one-day contract to pitch on the final day of the 1947 season to do what he said he could. He pitched four innings of shutout ball. Dean hurt himself sliding into second on a fielder's choice after reaching on a single in the bottom of the third inning. He did pitch the fourth inning but came out afterward due to the injury. Even at age 37 and having been away from the game for seven seasons he was still the "Great Dizzy Dean."

Missouri Historical Society, St. Louis

Inducted into the Hall of Fame as a player in 1953 by the BBWAA

Position: *Pitcher*

Batted: *Right* **Threw:** *Right*

Height: *6' 2"* **Weight:** *182 lbs.*

Born: *January 16, 1910, in Lucas, AR*

Died: *July 17, 1974, in Reno, NV*

Buried: *Bond Cemetery in Bond, MS*

Debut: *September 28, 1930, with the St. Louis Cardinals*

Final game: *September 28, 1947, with the St. Louis Browns*

Postseason: *World Series Champion (1934), 2x N.L. Pennant (1934, 1938)*

Awards & Recognition:
4× All-Star (1934–1937), N.L. MVP (1934)
2× MLB Wins Leader (1934, 1935),
4× MLB Strikeout Leader (1932–1935)

Nickname: *The Great Man*

Numbers worn in St. Louis:
Cardinals (17—retired), Browns (31)

Dizzy Dean – HOF Pitching Stats – WAR: 46.2

YEAR	TEAM	LG	W	L	ERA	G	CG	SHO	SV	IP	H	HR	BB	SO
1930	STL	NL	1	0	1.00	1	1	0	0	9	3	0	3	5
1932	STL	NL	18	15	3.30	46	16	4	2	286	280	14	102	191
1933	STL	NL	20	18	3.04	48	26	3	5	293	279	11	64	199
1934	STL	NL	30	7	2.66	50	24	7	7	311.2	288	14	75	195
1935	STL	NL	28	12	3.04	50	29	3	5	325.1	324	16	77	190
1936	STL	NL	24	13	3.17	51	28	2	11	315	310	21	53	195
1937	STL	NL	13	10	2.69	27	17	4	1	197.1	200	9	33	120
1938	CHC	NL	7	1	1.81	13	3	1	0	74.2	63	2	8	22
1939	CHC	NL	6	4	3.36	19	7	2	0	96.1	98	4	17	27
1940	CHC	NL	3	3	5.17	10	3	0	0	54	68	4	20	18
1941	CHC	NL	0	0	18.00	1	0	0	0	1	3	0	0	1
1947	SLB	AL	0	0	0.00	1	0	0	0	4	3	0	1	0
Career Totals			150	83	3.02	317	154	26	31	1967.1	1919	95	453	1163
STL (7 yrs)		NL	134	75	2.99	273	141	23	31	1737.1	1684	85	407	1095
SLB (1 yr)		AL	0	0	0.00	1	0	0	0	4	3	0	1	0

Getty Images

Bobby Wallace

Roderick "Bobby" Wallace began his career pitching alongside Cy Young on the N.L.'s Cleveland Spiders before becoming one of the game's best shortstops. Like Hall of Famers Burkett and Young, Wallace was reassigned to the St. Louis Perfectos as part of ownership's plan to put their best players in St. Louis in hopes of winning a pennant.

While just a decent hitter, Wallace was one of the games most agile and versatile players. His athleticism led him to shortstop, where he revolutionized the position. Shortstops at that time were using a three-step process of fielding the ball, straightening up, and finally throwing to first base. Too often speedy batters would beat the throw. That's where Wallace's play was different. Using his strong arm and outstanding range, Wallace would field and throw the ball in one continuous motion that soon set him apart from other defenders. His play earned him the nickname "Mr. Shortstop," a moniker also given to several future St. Louis shortstops.

In 1902, Wallace switched St. Louis teams, leaving his N.L. team that changed their name to the Cardinals to join the A.L. Browns in their second season.

The N.L. had a salary limit of $2,400 a year. The A.L. didn't, and since free agency ruled the game, he jumped to the Browns and signed a five-year contract worth $32,500—the highest in the game. Wallace had a good career with the Browns and in 1911 became their manager. He was, however, not cut out for that role and only lasted a year and a half. He stayed with the team another four seasons before going back to the Cardinals as a part-time player in 1917 and 1918. While Wallace's career would last 25 seasons he never played in the postseason, giving him the record for the longest career by a player who never played in a World Series.

Wikimedia Commons

Inducted into the Hall of Fame as a player in 1953 by the Veteran's Committee

Positions: *Shortstop, Pitcher, Manager*

Batted: *Right* **Threw:** *Right*

Height: *5' 8"* **Weight:** *170 lbs.*

Born: *November 4, 1873, in Pittsburgh, PA*

Died: *November 3, 1960, in Torrance, CA*

Buried: *Inglewood Park Cemetery in Inglewood CA*

Debut: *September 15, 1894, with the Cleveland Spiders*

Final game: *September 2, 1918, with the St. Louis Cardinals*

Postseason: *N/A*

Awards & Recognition: *N.L. Defensive WAR Leader (1901), 2× A.L. WAR Leader (1902, 1908)*

Number worn in St. Louis: *Played prior to numbers being worn*

Bobby Wallace – Career Managerial Stats

YEAR(S)	SEASONS	TEAM	LEAGUE	WON	LOST	W-L%	TIES	GAMES	EJECTIONS	PENNANTS	CHAMPIONSHIPS
1911 - 1912	2	SLB	AL	57	134	.298	1	192	0	0	0
1937	1	CIN	NL	5	20	.200	0	25	0	0	0
Career Totals	3			62	154	.287	1	217	0	0	0

Bobby Wallace – HOF Playing Stats – WAR: 76.4, Slash Line: .268 / .332 / .358

YEAR(S)	SEASONS	TEAM	LG	G	AB	R	H	2B	3B	HR	RBI	SB	BB	SO	BA
1894 - 1898	5	CLV	NL	363	1369	215	391	67	40	8	239	23	128	85	.286
1899 - 1901, 1917 - 1918	5	STL	NL	451	1720	233	494	88	38	18	275	40	120	82	.287
1902 - 1916	15	SLB	AL	1569	5529	609	1424	236	65	8	607	138	526	393	.258
Career Totals	25			2383	8618	1057	2309	391	143	34	1121	201	774	560	.268

Rabbit Maranville

Walter Maranville was nicknamed "Rabbit" because, as he told it, that's how a friend's younger sister described his style of play on the field. She said, "you hop and bound around like one." And it was that style of play at shortstop that would take Maranville all the way to the Hall of Fame. While only a .258 career hitter, the "Rabbit" was one of the game's best defensive shortstops in the 1920s.

While a standout on the field, he is also identified as one of the game's unique characters and unusual personalities. Well known for his many stunts and practical jokes, Maranville could definitely play the game, and he did so for 23 seasons—all in the N.L., a record that would last until broken by Pete Rose in 1986. Fifteen of those years were spent with the Boston Braves, where he began his career in 1912. He helped the Braves to the 1914 pennant and a four-game sweep of the Athletics in that year's World Series, in which Maranville batted .308.

Interestingly, Maranville would also hit .308 in his only other World Series appearance. That occurred in 1928 as the everyday shortstop with the St. Louis Cardinals. It was a season in which he almost didn't play. After 13 seasons in the big leagues, Maranville had become a washed-up part-time player in 1925, bouncing between three teams—the last being the Cardinals, who had signed him to a minor league contract in 1927. During that season he freed himself of the "demons of the bottle," and in 1928 he finished 10th in the MVP voting while helping the Cardinals win the pennant.

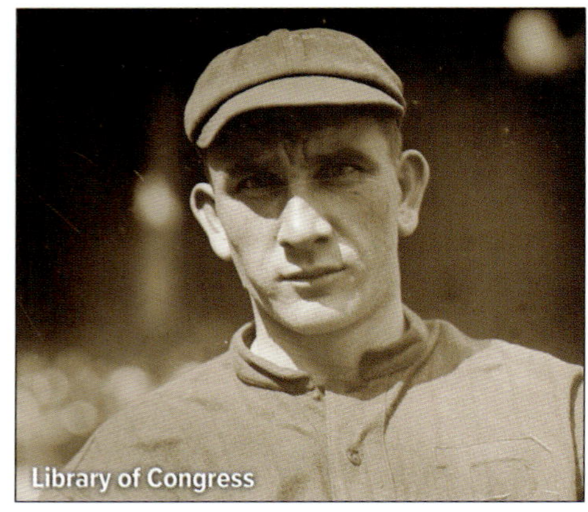
Library of Congress

Inducted into the Hall of Fame as a player in 1954 by the BBWAA

Positions: *Shortstop, Second Base, Manager*

Batted: *Right* **Threw:** *Right*

Height: *5' 5"* **Weight:** *155 lbs.*

Born: *November 11, 1891, in Springfield, MA*

Died: *January 6, 1954, in Woodside, NY*

Buried: *St. Michael Cemetery, Springfield, MA*

Debut: *September 10, 1912, with the Boston Braves*

Final game: *September 29, 1935, with the Boston Braves*

Postseason: *1x World Series Champion (1914), 2x N.L. Pennant Winner (1914, 1928)*

Awards & Recognition: *3× N.L. Defensive WAR Leader (1914, 1916, 1920)*

Number worn in St. Louis: *Played prior to numbers being worn*

Rabbit Maranville – Career Managerial Stats

YEAR(S)	SEASONS	TEAM	LEAGUE	WON	LOST	W-L%	TIES	GAMES	EJECTIONS	PENNANTS	CHAMPIONSHIPS
1914	1	CHC	NL	23	30	.434	0	53	0	0	0
Career Totals	**1**			**23**	**30**	**.434**	**0**	**53**	**0**	**0**	**0**

Rabbit Maranville – HOF Playing Stats – WAR: 44.0, Slash Line: .258 / .318 / .340

YEAR(S)	SEASONS	TEAM	LG	G	AB	R	H	2B	3B	HR	RBI	SB	BB	SO	BA
1912 - 1920, 1929 - 1933, 1935	15	BSN	NL	1795	6724	802	1696	244	103	23	558	194	561	515	.252
1921 - 1924	4	PIT	NL	601	2459	345	697	103	56	4	245	81	185	168	.283
1925	1	CHC	NL	75	266	37	62	10	3	0	23	6	29	20	.233
1926	1	BRO	NL	78	234	32	55	8	5	0	24	7	26	24	.235
1927-1928	**2**	**STL**	**NL**	**121**	**395**	**40**	**95**	**15**	**10**	**1**	**34**	**3**	**38**	**29**	**.241**
Career Totals	**23**			**2670**	**10078**	**1256**	**2605**	**380**	**177**	**28**	**884**	**291**	**839**	**756**	**.258**

Library of Congress

Dazzy Vance

Charles Vance was one of baseball's premier pitchers during the 1920s. His "dazzling" fastball earned him the nickname "Dazzy" while striking out batters one after another. For seven straight years with Brooklyn's Robins, Vance was the N.L. strikeout leader. In 1924 he won the N.L. MVP after posting a pitching triple crown. That year Vance had more strikeouts than the second- and third-place pitchers combined. Despite his heroics on the mound, the World Series eluded Vance through his first 14 seasons and seemed unlikely to ever happen.

Vance left his first career start in Pittsburgh in 1915 with arm issues. Traded to the Yankees, he lost three more times before being sent down. He bounced around the minors before another call up in 1918 and two unimpressive outings. After four seasons, Vance was yet to record a win in 11 big league games, with only 18 strikeouts to go along with three hit batters and 24 walks.

He was back in the minors and in pain until successful surgery returned the "dazzle" of the past and put Vance back in the big leagues with Brooklyn. At age 41 in 1932, Vance posted double-digit wins once more. He was traded to the Cardinals the following year but delivered an underwhelming season of only six wins.

The Reds claimed Vance off waivers to start the 1934 season, but after he lost two of the six games he pitched, a mid-season waiver claim brought Vance back to the Cardinals to become a member of the pennant-winning Gas House Gang. He pitched in 19 games before going to the World Series and pitched an inning-and-a-half in a 10–4 Game Four loss. He then finished his career back in Brooklyn, pitching from their bullpen to close one of baseball's most dazzling careers.

Inducted into the Hall of Fame as a player in 1955 by the BBWAA

Positions: *Pitcher*

Batted: *Right* **Threw:** *Right*

Height: *6' 2"* **Weight:** *200 lbs.*

Born: *March 4, 1891, in Orient, IA*

Died: *February 16, 1961, in Homosassa Springs, FL*

Buried: *Stage Stand Cemetery, Homosassa Springs, FL*

Debut: *April 16, 1915, with the Pittsburgh Pirates*

Final game: *August 14, 1935, with the Brooklyn Dodgers*

Postseason: *World Series Champion (1934), N.L. Pennant (1934)*

Awards & Recognition: *N.L. MVP (1924), Pitching Triple Crown (1924), 2× MLB Wins Leader (1924, 1925), 3× N.L. ERA Leader (1924, 1928, 1930), 7× N.L. Strikeout Leader (1922–1928), Pitched No-hitter on September 13, 1925*

Number worn in St. Louis: *Cardinals (19)*

Dazzy Vance – HOF Pitching Stats – WAR: 60.3

YEAR	TEAM	LG	W	L	ERA	G	CG	SHO	SV	IP	H	HR	BB	SO
1915	PIT	NL	0	1	10.13	1	0	0	0	2.2	3	0	5	0
1915	NYY	AL	0	3	3.54	8	1	0	0	28	23	1	16	18
1918	NYY	AL	0	0	15.43	2	0	0	0	2.1	9	0	2	0
1922	BRO	NL	18	12	3.70	36	17	5	0	245.2	259	9	94	134
1923	BRO	NL	18	15	3.50	37	21	3	0	280.1	263	10	100	197
1924	BRO	NL	28	6	2.16	35	30	3	0	308.1	238	11	77	262
1925	BRO	NL	22	9	3.53	31	26	4	0	265.1	247	8	66	221
1926	BRO	NL	9	10	3.89	24	12	0	1	169	172	7	58	140
1927	BRO	NL	16	15	2.70	34	25	2	1	273.1	242	12	69	184
1928	BRO	NL	22	10	2.09	38	24	4	2	280.1	226	11	72	200
1929	BRO	NL	14	13	3.89	31	17	1	0	231.1	244	15	47	126
1930	BRO	NL	17	15	2.61	35	20	4	1	258.2	241	15	55	173
1931	BRO	NL	11	13	3.38	30	12	2	0	218.2	221	12	53	150
1932	BRO	NL	12	11	4.20	27	9	1	1	175.2	171	10	57	103
1933	**STL**	**NL**	**6**	**2**	**3.55**	**28**	**2**	**0**	**3**	**99**	**105**	**3**	**28**	**67**
1934	TOT	NL	1	3	4.56	25	1	0	1	77	90	5	25	42
1934	CIN	NL	0	2	7.50	6	0	0	0	18	28	1	11	9
1934	**STL**	**NL**	**1**	**1**	**3.66**	**19**	**1**	**0**	**1**	**59**	**62**	**4**	**14**	**33**
1935	BRO	NL	3	2	4.41	20	0	0	2	51	55	3	16	28
Career Totals			**197**	**140**	**3.24**	**442**	**217**	**29**	**12**	**2966.2**	**2809**	**132**	**840**	**2045**
STL (2 yrs)		**NL**	**7**	**3**	**3.59**	**47**	**3**	**0**	**4**	**158**	**167**	**7**	**42**	**100**

Getty Images

Bill McKechnie

Bill McKechnie's spent 11 uneventful years playing for six teams in the major leagues and the Federal League. His .251 hitting with only eight home runs was not Hall of Fame caliber, but his 25 seasons managing five different teams and winning four pennants and two World Series Championships met the mark. One of those pennants was with the St. Louis Cardinals.

McKechnie's mantra was simple: pitching and defense are the backbone of winning. Using that philosophy, McKechnie became the first manager to win pennants with three different N.L. clubs: the Pittsburgh Pirates (1925), St. Louis Cardinals (1928) and Cincinnati Reds (1939 and 1940). His managerial career began as a player–manager in the Federal League in 1915. He wouldn't manage in the majors until 1922 with the Pirates. Within four seasons he had given Pittsburgh a World Championship. Internal disputes led to McKechnie's departure after the 1926 season. But winners bounce back, and McKechnie landed in St. Louis in 1927 as a coach-turned-manager in 1928. He led the Cardinals to their second pennant in three years. The Yankees swept McKechnie's Redbirds in four games to avenge the Cardinals 1926 Fall Classic win. Cardinals owner Sam Breadon was so embarrassed he demoted McKechnie to the minors and brought up Billy Southworth to manage the team in 1929. The team tumbled and Breadon realized his mistake, swapping the two skippers at mid-season. The damage, however, was done. While rebounding under McKechnie, the team could do no better than fourth place.

McKechnie decided he was done in St. Louis and accepted a four-year contract to manage the Boston Braves in 1930. In 1938 he went to Cincinnati for an eight-year stint that delivered two pennants and another World Championship. When he retired from managing in 1946, his 1,896 N.L. victories were second only to John McGraw's 2,669.

Library of Congress

Inducted into the Hall of Fame as a manager in 1962 by the Veterans Committee

Positions: *Third Base, Manager*

Batted: *Both* **Threw:** *Right*

Height: *5′ 10″* **Weight:** *160 lbs.*

Born: *August 7, 1886, in Wilkinsburg, PA*

Died: *October 29, 1965, in Bradenton, FL*

Buried: *Manasota Memorial Park, Bradenton, FL*

Debut: *September 8, 1907, with the Pittsburgh Pirates*

Final game: *September 20, 1920, with the Pittsburgh Pirates*

Postseason: *2× World Series Champion (1925, 1940) 4× N.L. Pennant (1925, 1928, 1939, 1940)*

Nickname: *Deacon*

Number worn in St. Louis: *Played prior to numbers being worn*

Bill McKechnie – HOF Career Managerial Stats

YEAR(S)	SEASONS	TEAM	LEAGUE	WON	LOST	W-L%	TIES	GAMES	EJECTIONS	PENNANTS	CHAMPIONSHIPS
1915	1	NEW	FL	54	45	.545	3	102	3	0	0
1922 - 1926	5	PIT	NL	409	293	.583	5	707	10	1	1
1928 - 1929	**2**	**STL**	**NL**	**129**	**88**	**.594**	**0**	**217**	**2**	**1**	**0**
1930 - 1937	8	BSN	NL	560	666	.457	9	1235	11	0	0
1938 - 1946	9	CIN	NL	744	631	.541	11	1386	6	2	1
Career Totals	**25**			**1896**	**1723**	**.524**	**28**	**3647**	**32**	**4**	**2**

Bill McKechnie – Career Playing Stats – WAR: 3.3, Slash Line: .251 / .301 / .313

YEAR(S)	SEASONS	TEAM	LEAGUE	G	AB	R	H	2B	3B	HR	RBI	SB	BB	SO	BA
1907, 1910 - 1912, 1919, 1920	6	PIT	NL	368	1182	118	278	25	20	5	109	34	71	80	.235
1913	1	BSN	NL	1	4	1	0	0	0	0	0	0	0	1	.000
1913	1	NYY	AL	45	112	7	15	0	0	0	8	2	8	17	.134
1914	1	IND	FL	149	570	107	173	24	6	2	38	47	53	36	.304
1915	1	NEW	FL	127	451	49	113	22	5	1	43	28	41	31	.251
1916	1	NYG	NL	71	260	22	64	9	1	0	17	7	7	20	.246
1916 - 1917	2	CIN	NL	85	264	15	70	6	1	0	25	9	10	19	.265
Career Totals	**11**			**846**	**2843**	**319**	**713**	**86**	**33**	**8**	**240**	**127**	**190**	**204**	**.251**

Library of Congress

Burleigh Grimes

Burleigh Grimes used a little extra on his pitches while winning 270 big league games. When the spitball was banned in February 1920, Grimes was one of 16 pitchers allowed to continue throwing the pitch. Doctoring the ball with his salivary concoction resulted in an erratic break on the ball that baffled hitters.

Grimes bounced between seven teams during his 19 seasons in the big leagues. He played in four World Series between his first and final games in Pittsburgh. He had a nine-year run with Brooklyn that included a trip to 1920's Fall Classic against Cleveland, in which Grimes went 1–2. He was traded to the New York Giants in 1927 and won 13 in a row during a 19–8 season. After rubbing Giants skipper John McGraw the wrong way, Grimes was shipped back to Pittsburgh and led the majors in wins, complete games, and innings pitched. Following a contract dispute he was traded to the Braves but lasted only 11 games before joining a Cardinal team that would win two straight pennants during Grimes's two-year stay.

Squaring off against Connie Mack's Athletics in both Series, Grimes was 0–2 in the A's six-game win in 1930. A year later Grimes's two wins gave the Cardinals a Series win in seven games. His Game Seven win was one of the gutsiest in World Series history. In extreme pain and suffering through an appendicitis attack, Grimes pitched eight innings of shutout ball before weakening. He gave up two runs and was unable to finish the ninth. The Cardinals got the final out and the win. They traded Grimes to the Cubs the next season to make room for Dizzy Dean. Grimes was winless in the 1932 World Series as the Yankees swept the Cubs. Nearing the end of his career, Grimes was released and rejoined the Redbirds in 1933. Released by the Cardinals in 1934, Grimes finished the year and his career with the Yankees and Pirates as baseball's last legal spitballer in 1934.

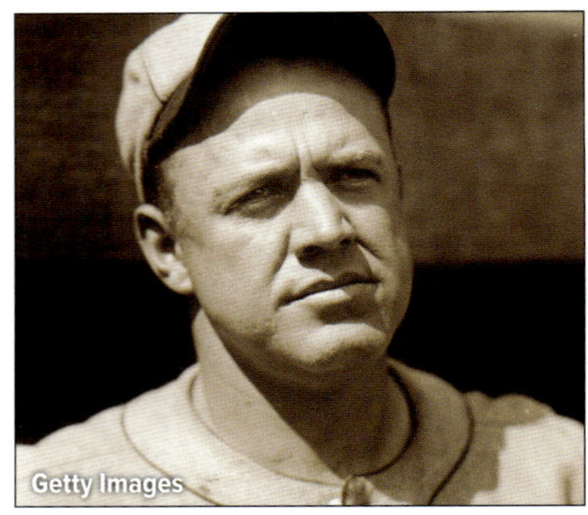
Getty Images

Inducted into the Hall of Fame as a player in 1964 by the Veterans Committee

Positions: *Pitcher, Manager*

Batted: *Right* **Threw:** *Right*

Height: *5' 10"* **Weight:** *175 lbs.*

Born: *August 18, 1893, in Emerald, WI*

Died: *December 6, 1985, in Clear Lake, WI*

Buried: *Clear Lake Cemetery, Clear Lake, WI*

Debut: *September 10, 1916, with the Pittsburgh Pirates*

Final game: *September 20, 1934, with the Pittsburgh Pirates*

Postseason: *World Series Champion (1931), 4× N.L. Pennant (1920, 1930, 1931, 1932)*

Awards & Recognition: *2× N.L. Wins Leader (1921, 1928), N.L. Strikeout Leader (1921)*

Nickname: *Ol' Stubblebeard*

Number worn in St. Louis: *Cardinals (20)*

Burleigh Grimes – Career Managerial Stats

YEAR(S)	SEASONS	TEAM	LEAGUE	WON	LOST	W-L%	TIES	GAMES	EJECTIONS	PENNANTS	CHAMPIONSHIPS
1937 - 1938	2	BRO	NL	131	171	.434	4	306	15	0	0

Burleigh Grimes – HOF Career Playing Stats – WAR: 52.9

YEAR(S)	SEASONS	TEAM	LEAGUE	W	L	ERA	G	CG	SHO	SV	IP	H	HR	BB	SO
1916 - 1917, 1928 - 1929, 1934	5	PIT	NL	48	42	3.26	132	58	7	5	830.1	818	28	237	260
1918 - 1926	9	BRO	NL	158	121	3.46	318	205	20	5	2426	2547	76	744	952
1927	1	NYG	NL	19	8	3.54	39	15	2	2	259.2	274	12	87	102
1930	1	BSN	NL	3	5	7.35	11	1	0	0	49	72	4	22	15
1930 - 1931, 1933 -1934	**4**	**STL**	**NL**	**32**	**17**	**3.45**	**59**	**27**	**4**	**1**	**386**	**434**	**18**	**112**	**130**
1932 - 1933	2	CHC	NL	9	17	4.35	47	8	2	4	211	245	10	79	48
1934	1	NYY	AL	1	2	5.50	10	0	0	1	18	22	0	14	5
Career Totals	**19**			**270**	**212**	**3.53**	**616**	**314**	**35**	**18**	**4180**	**4412**	**148**	**1295**	**1512**

Getty Images

Miller Huggins

St. Louis's loss became New York's gain. Miller Huggins spent eight seasons with the Cardinals as a player (1910–16) and a manager (1913–1917). He only left after his offer to buy the Cardinals was passed over during the team's ownership change following the 1917 season. A disillusioned Miller headed to the Yankees and won six pennants and three World Championships before his premature death in 1929 at age 51. How many more titles could he have won with the Bronx Bombers had he not died so young? If he had stayed in St. Louis, would he have had the same Hall of Fame career?

As a player, the diminutive five-foot-six-inch Huggins was a pesky .265 hitter who always found a way to get on base. Four times during his 13-year career he led the league in walks. In 1910 he put his name in the record books by recording six plate appearances and no official at-bats—he collected four walks and two sacrifice flies. In 1911 the sure-handed second baseman tied the N.L. record for successful fielding chances in a game with 16 and finished sixth in the voting for the Chalmers Award for Most Valuable Player.

But it wasn't his playing career that got him in the Hall of Fame—it was his managerial skills. The law school graduate had an astute baseball mind committed to the fundamentals of the game. As a Cardinals manager he never won a pennant. His highest finish was third, which to that point was the team's highest finish since entering the N.L. In New York, Huggins's time was all about winning, which wasn't too hard when your lineup was known as "Murderers Row" and included Ruth, Gehrig, Lazzeri, and other feared hitters. Huggins's biggest challenge was simply keeping Babe Ruth in line.

Library of Congress

Inducted into the Hall of Fame as a manager in 1964 by the Veterans Committee

Position: *Second base*

Batted: *Both* **Threw:** *Right*

Height: *5' 6"* **Weight:** *140 lbs.*

Born: *March 27, 1878, in Cincinnati, OH*

Died: *September 25, 1929, in New York, NY*

Buried: *Spring Grove Cemetery, Cincinnati, OH*

Debut: *April 15, 1904, with the Cincinnati Reds*

Final game: *September 13, 1916, with the St. Louis Cardinals*

Postseason: *3× World Series Champion (1923, 1927, 1928) 6x A.L. Pennants (1921–1923, 1926–1928)*

Nicknames: *Hug, Mighty Mite*

Number worn in St. Louis: *Played prior to numbers being worn*

Miller Huggins – HOF Career Managerial Stats

YEAR(S)	SEASONS	TEAM	LEAGUE	WON	LOST	W-L%	TIES	GAMES	EJECTIONS	PENNANTS	CHAMPIONSHIPS
1913 - 1917	**5**	**STL**	**NL**	**346**	**415**	**.455**	**13**	**774**	**12**	**0**	**0**
1918 - 1929	12	NYY	AL	1067	719	.597	10	1796	14	6	3
Career Totals	**17**			**1413**	**1134**	**.555**	**23**	**2570**	**26**	**6**	**3**

Miller Huggins – Career Playing Stats – WAR: 35.4, Slash Line: .265 / .382 / .314

YEAR(S)	SEASONS	TEAM	LEAGUE	G	AB	R	H	2B	3B	HR	RBI	SB	BB	SO	BA
1904 - 1909	6	CIN	NL	783	2818	441	734	63	32	4	154	150	431	244	.260
1910 - 1916	**7**	**STL**	**NL**	**803**	**2740**	**507**	**740**	**83**	**18**	**5**	**164**	**174**	**572**	**312**	**.270**
Career Totals	**13**			**1586**	**5558**	**948**	**1474**	**146**	**50**	**9**	**318**	**324**	**1003**	**556**	**.265**

Library of Congress

Pud Galvin

In 1888 James Francis "Pud" Galvin became baseball's first pitcher to win 300 games. He was called "Pud" due to his uncanny ability to make hitters look like "pudding," although others believe it was due to his pudgy physique. His 15-year, 365-game-winning career began and ended in St. Louis. Ironically, his first and last seasons were the only two he played in the city where he was born and raised.

Galvin first pitched for the St. Louis Brown Stockings of the National Association (N.A.) in 1875. A season later the team joined the newly formed N.L. Galvin didn't stay with them. He instead played three years with the St. Louis Red Stockings, a former N.A. franchise that continued playing as an unaffiliated team across the country. August 17, 1876, was a memorable day in Galvin's career. That day in the first game of a tournament in Ionia, Michigan, he threw a no-hitter against a team from Detroit. In the second game Galvin threw the first recorded perfect game in baseball history, against a different Detroit team.

Galvin finally made it to the N.L. in 1879 with the Buffalo Bisons and soon became a workhorse. He pitched in 66 of the team's 78 games, winning 37 times. In seven years with the team, he won an amazing 218 games. He then pitched for a year and a half in the A.A. before returning to the N.L. to win 156 games in seven years with the N.L.'s Pittsburgh Alleghenys (today's Pirates). In June of 1892, he was traded to his hometown St. Louis Browns (today's Cardinals) to finish his career. It was a record-setting career, but a career in which he never appeared in a World Series. He remains the only pitcher to win 20 or more games 10 times and never win a pennant.

Getty Images

Inducted into the Hall of Fame as a player in 1965 by the Veterans Committee

Positions: *Pitcher, Manager*

Batted: *Right* **Threw:** *Right*

Height: *5' 8"* **Weight:** *180 lbs.*

Born: *December 25, 1856, in St. Louis, MO*

Died: *March 7, 1902, in Pittsburgh, PA*

Buried: *Calvary Cemetery, Pittsburgh, PA*

Debut: *May 33, 1875, with the St. Louis Brown Stockings*

Final game: *August 2, 1892, with the N.L. St. Louis Browns*

Postseason: *N/A*

Awards & Recognition: *Baseball's first 300 game winner, 3× No-hitters (1876, 1880, 1884) Perfect Game (1876)*

Nickname: *Pud*

Number worn in St. Louis: *Played prior to numbers being worn*

Pud Galvin – Career Managerial Stats

YEAR(S)	SEASONS	TEAM	LEAGUE	WON	LOST	W-L%	TIES	GAMES	EJECTIONS	PENNANTS	CHAMPIONSHIPS
1885	1	BUF	NL	7	17	.292	0	24	0	0	0
Career Totals	**1**			**7**	**17**	**.292**	**0**	**24**	**0**	**0**	**0**

Pud Galvin – HOF Career Playing Stats – WAR: 73.4

YEAR(S)	SEASONS	TM	LG	W	L	ERA	G	CG	SHO	SV	IP	H	HR	BB	SO
1875	**1**	**STL**	**NA**	**4**	**2**	**1.16**	**8**	**7**	**0**	**1**	**62**	**53**	**0**	**1**	**8**
1879 - 1885	7	BUF	NL	218	179	2.63	413	381	39	1	3547.2	3733	60	299	1303
1885 - 1889, 1891 - 1892	7	PIT	AA	126	110	3.10	246	225	17	0	2084.2	2242	54	370	434
1890	1	PBB	PL	12	13	4.35	26	23	1	0	217	275	3	49	35
1892	**1**	**STL**	**NL**	**5**	**6**	**3.23**	**12**	**10**	**0**	**0**	**92**	**102**	**4**	**26**	**27**
Career Totals	**15**			**365**	**310**	**2.85**	**705**	**646**	**57**	**2**	**6003**	**6405**	**121**	**745**	**1807**

Library of Congress

Branch Rickey

Before creating a legacy with the Cardinals, the Dodgers, and finally the Pirates, Branch Rickey was a player, manager, and team president with the St. Louis Browns. Rickey spent four seasons as a catcher, and he wasn't a particularly good one. Playing with a sore arm for the New York Highlanders, he set a record one day in June 1907 when he allowed 13 runners to steal bases in a single game. But he wasn't selected for the Hall of Fame because of his play; he was inducted as an executive. Rickey would manage the Browns and Cardinals for 10 years before putting his true baseball skill to use. That skill was identifying and developing baseball talent. Unfortunately, Browns owner Phil Ball didn't buy into it, but Rickey's new boss, Cardinals owner Sam Breadon, did. In a day when major league teams would bid against each other for minor league players (they had no minor league affiliations), Rickey knew he could find, sign, and develop good talent. He became the father of baseball's first farm system with the Cardinals. It was the envy of, and model for, all other teams. But because Rickey did it first, the Cardinals reaped the rewards. They won six pennants before Rickey jumped to Brooklyn after the 1942 season. The seeds of the Cardinal system would produce three additional pennants in the four years after he left. Brownie fans always wondered what would have happened if their owner had allowed Rickey to foster the minor leagues within their franchise.

In Brooklyn, Rickey continued his groundbreaking ways. Under his tutelage the Dodgers began using batting cages, pitching machines, and batting helmets—things we take for granted today. He even hired a statistician to optimize the team's play through statistics. But Rickey's most revolutionary accomplishment was the Dodgers' signing of Jackie Robinson to break baseball's color barrier in April 1947. He may not have been a great baseball talent on the field, but it's hard argue that anyone impacted the game off the field more than Branch Rickey.

Getty Images

Inducted into the Hall of Fame as a pioneer/executive in 1967 by the Veterans Committee

Positions: *Catcher, Left Field, First Base, Manager, Executive*

Batted: *Left* **Threw:** *Right*

Height: *5' 9"* **Weight:** *175 lbs.*

Born: *December 29, 1891, in Portsmouth, OH*

Died: *December 9, 1965, in Columbia, MO*

Buried: *Rushtown Cemetery, Rushtown, OH*

Debut: *June 16, 1905, with the St. Louis Browns*

Final game: *August 25, 1914, with the St. Louis Browns*

Postseason: *4× World Series Champion (Executive—1926, 1931, 1934, 1942) 8× N.L. Pennant (Executive—1926, 1928, 1930, 1931, 1934, 1942, 1947, 1949)*

Awards & Recognition: *Spearheaded the integration of baseball*

Nickname: *The Mahatma*

Number worn in St. Louis: *Played prior to numbers being worn*

Branch Rickey – Career HOF Pioneer / Executive Stats

YEAR(S)	SEASONS	TEAM	LEAGUE	WON	LOST	W-L%	TIES	GAMES	PENNANTS	CHAMPIONSHIPS
1913 - 1916	4	SLB	AL	270	344	.428	17.000	631	0	0
1917 - 1942	26	STL	NL	2165	1781	.544	34.000	3980	6	4
1943 - 1950	8	BRO	NL	691	542	.557	8.000	1241	2	0
1950 - 1955	6	PIT	NL	326	597	.352	3	926	0	0
Career Totals	44			3452	3264	.509	62.000	6778	8	4

Branch Rickey – Career Managerial Stats

YEAR(S)	SEASONS	TEAM	LEAGUE	WON	LOST	W-L%	TIES	GAMES	EJECTIONS	PENNANTS	CHAMPIONSHIPS
1913 - 1915	3	SLB	AL	139	179	.437	12	330	2	0	0
1919 - 1925	7	STL	NL	458	485	.486	4	947	1	0	0
Career Totals	10			597	664	.473	16	1277	3	0	0

Branch Rickey – Career Playing Stats – WAR: 0.6, Slash Line: .239 / .304 / .324

YEAR(S)	SEASONS	TEAM	LEAGUE	G	AB	R	H	2B	3B	HR	RBI	SB	BB	SO	BA
1905 - 1906, 1914	3	SLB	AL	68	206	22	57	7	3	3	24	4	16	29	.277
1907	1	NYY	AL	52	137	16	25	1	3	0	15	4	11	25	.182
Career Totals	4			120	343	38	82	8	6	3	39	8	27	54	.239

Library of Congress

Joe Medwick

Between 1932 and 1942, Joe Medwick's batting average never dipped below .300. The dangerous hitter spent nine of those seasons with the Cardinals, including 1937, when he won the Triple Crown and MVP award—a feat yet to be repeated in the N.L. Six of his 10 All-Star appearances came in a St. Louis uniform, as did his lone World Series Championship in 1934.

That was a Series to remember. Medwick opened the Series with four straight hits, including a home run, as the Gas House Gang Cardinals hammered the Detroit Tigers 8–3. Medwick would hit .379 in the seven-game Fall Classic. Known for his hard-nosed style and competitive nature, the cantankerous Medwick ignited one of World Series history's most interesting incidents. With a 7–0 lead in Game Seven's sixth inning and 30-game winner Dizzy Dean cruising on the mound, Medwick came to bat with two out and a man on second. He drilled a ball off the right field wall and headed for third sliding hard for the base, where the Tigers' third baseman met Medwick's slide by digging his spiked foot into Joe's leg. Medwick retaliated, and a melee ensued. Once play resumed and Medwick trotted out to left field, the Detroit fans greeted him with a chorus of boos and thrown fruit and soda bottles. Play was held up while the debris was cleaned, and every time Medwick tried to take his position more items flew toward him. Eventually, the commissioner removed Medwick "to protect the player from injury and permit the game to proceed." And it did. The Cardinals won 11–0.

Tired of Medwick's personality and contract squabbles, Cardinal leadership traded him to Brooklyn in mid-season 1940. He would appear in two more All-Star games and the 1941 World Series with the Dodgers before ending his career back with the Cardinals in 1947 and 1948.

Inducted into the Hall of Fame as a player in 1968 by the BBWAA

Position: *Left Field*

Batted: *Right* **Threw:** *Right*

Height: *5' 10"* **Weight:** *187 lbs.*

Born: *November 24, 1911, in Carteret, NJ*

Died: *March 21, 1975, in St. Petersburgh, FL*

Buried: *St. Lucas Cemetery, Sunset Hills, MO*

Debut: *September 2, 1932, with the St. Louis Cardinals*

Final game: *July 25, 1948, with the St. Louis Cardinals*

Postseason: *1x World Series Champion (1934) 2x N.L. Pennant (1934, 1941)*

Awards & Recognition: *10× All-Star (1934–1942, 1944), N.L. MVP (1937), Triple Crown (1937), N.L. Batting Leader 1937, N.L. Home Run Leader (1937), 3× N.L. RBI Leader (1936–1938*

Nicknames: *Ducky, Muscles*

Numbers worn in St. Louis: *Cardinals (28, 7, 21, 12)*

Joe Medwick HOF Playing Stats – WAR: 54.5, Slash Line: .324 / .362 / .505

YEAR	TEAM	LG	G	AB	R	H	2B	3B	HR	RBI	SB	BB	SO	BA
1932	STL	NL	26	106	13	37	12	1	2	12	3	2	10	.349
1933	STL	NL	148	595	92	182	40	10	18	98	5	26	56	.306
1934	STL	NL	149	620	110	198	40	18	18	106	3	21	83	.319
1935	STL	NL	154	634	132	224	46	13	23	126	4	30	59	.353
1936	STL	NL	155	636	115	223	64	13	18	138	3	34	33	.351
1937	STL	NL	156	633	111	237	56	10	31	154	4	41	50	.374
1938	STL	NL	146	590	100	190	47	8	21	122	0	42	41	.322
1939	STL	NL	150	606	98	201	48	8	14	117	6	45	44	.332
1940	STL	NL	37	158	21	48	12	0	3	20	0	6	8	.304
1940	BRO	NL	106	423	62	127	18	12	14	66	2	26	28	.300
1941	BRO	NL	133	538	100	171	33	10	18	88	2	38	35	.318
1942	BRO	NL	142	553	69	166	37	4	4	96	2	32	25	.300
1943	BRO	NL	48	173	13	47	10	0	0	25	1	10	8	.272
1943	NYG	NL	78	324	41	91	20	3	5	45	0	9	14	.281
1944	NYG	NL	128	490	64	165	24	3	7	85	2	38	24	.337
1945	NYG	NL	26	92	14	28	4	0	3	11	2	2	2	.304
1945	BSN	NL	66	218	17	62	13	0	0	26	3	12	12	.284
1946	BRO	NL	41	77	7	24	4	0	2	18	0	6	5	.312
1947	STL	NL	75	150	19	46	12	0	4	28	0	16	12	.307
1948	STL	NL	20	19	0	4	0	0	0	2	0	1	2	.211
Career Totals			1984	7635	1198	2471	540	113	205	1383	42	437	551	.324
STL (11 Yrs)		NL	1216	4747	811	1590	377	81	152	923	28	264	398	.335

Wikimedia Commons

Stan Musial

Considered the greatest Cardinal of all time, Stan Musial spent his entire 22-season career playing in St. Louis. He is remembered as one of the greatest and most consistent hitters the game has ever seen. This first-ballot Hall of Famer recorded a lifetime batting average of .331 on 3,630 career hits. Amazingly, 1,815 of his hits came at home, and 1,815 came on the road. When this seven-time NL batting champion retired, he held or shared 17 MLB, 29 N.L., and nine All-Star Game records. Most significantly, at his retirement, he was the MLB career leader in extra-base hits (1,377) and total bases (6,134). He was the NL leader for career hits (3,630), runs batted in (1,951), games played (3,026), at bats (10,972), runs scored (1,949), and doubles (725). His 475 home runs ranked second in N.L. history when he retired. One can only wonder how many more home runs Stan would have hit if Sportsman's Park did not have a screen running across right field, from the top of the wall to the Pavilion roof—not to mention that he spent the 1945 season serving in the Navy.

How fearful were his opponents and their fans of his hitting prowess? In 1946 Brooklyn fans were so weary of the Dodgers' inability to get Stan out, they began chanting during a game, "O-h-h, here comes the man again." As legendary sportswriter Bob Broeg wrote, it was not "that man," but "the man" out of respect, and thus Stan was forever honored with that nickname. Sixty-one seasons after his last game, only Pete Rose, Ty Cobb, and Hank Aaron have more hits than Stan Musial. To further highlight his impact on the game, only Aaron, Barry Bonds, and Albert Pujols have more career extra base hits than Stan.

Wikimedia Commons

Inducted into the Hall of Fame as a Player in 1969 (first ballot) by the BBWAA

Positions: *Outfield, First Base*

Batted: *Left* **Threw:** *Left*

Height: *6' 0"* **Weight:** *175*

Born: *November 21, 1920, in Donora, PA*

Died: *January 19, 2013, in Ladue, MO*

Buried: *Forever Bellerive Cemetery, Creve Coeur, MO*

Debut: *September 17, 1941, with the St. Louis Cardinals*

Last Game: *September 29, 1963, with the St. Louis Cardinals*

Postseason: *3× World Series Champion (1942, 1944, 1946), 4x N.L. Pennant (1942–1944, 1946)*

Awards & Recognition: *24× All-Star (1943, 1944, 1946–1963), 3× NL MVP (1943, 1946, 1948), 7× NL batting champion (1943, 1946, 1948, 1950–1952, 1957), 2× NL RBI leader (1948, 1956)*

Nickname: *The Man*

Number worn in St. Louis: *Cardinals (6—retired)*

Stan Musial – HOF Career Playing Stats – WAR: 128.5, Slash Line: .331 / .417 / .559

YEAR	TEAM	LG	G	AB	R	H	2B	3B	HR	RBI	BB	SO	BA
1941	STL	NL	12	47	8	20	4	0	1	7	2	1	.426
1942	STL	NL	140	467	87	147	32	10	10	72	62	25	.315
1943	STL	NL	157	617	108	220	48	20	13	81	72	18	.357
1944	STL	NL	146	568	112	197	51	14	12	94	90	28	.347
1945	Did not play in major or minor leagues (Military Service)												
1946	STL	NL	156	624	124	228	50	20	16	103	73	31	.365
1947	STL	NL	149	587	113	183	30	13	19	95	80	24	.312
1948	STL	NL	155	611	135	230	46	18	39	131	79	34	.376
1949	STL	NL	157	612	128	207	41	13	36	123	107	38	.338
1950	STL	NL	146	555	105	192	41	7	28	109	87	36	.346
1951	STL	NL	152	578	124	205	30	12	32	108	98	40	.355
1952	STL	NL	154	578	105	194	42	6	21	91	96	29	.336
1953	STL	NL	157	593	127	200	53	9	30	113	105	32	.337
1954	STL	NL	153	591	120	195	41	9	35	126	103	39	.330
1955	STL	NL	154	562	97	179	30	5	33	108	80	39	.319
1956	STL	NL	156	594	87	184	33	6	27	109	75	39	.310
1957	STL	NL	134	502	82	176	38	3	29	102	66	34	.351
1958	STL	NL	135	472	64	159	35	2	17	62	72	26	.337
1959	STL	NL	115	341	37	87	13	2	14	44	60	25	.255
1960	STL	NL	116	331	49	91	17	1	17	63	41	34	.275
1961	STL	NL	123	372	46	107	22	4	15	70	52	35	.288
1962	STL	NL	135	433	57	143	18	1	19	82	64	46	.330
1963	STL	NL	124	337	34	86	10	2	12	58	35	43	.255
Career Totals		NL	3026	10972	1949	3630	725	177	475	1951	1599	696	.331

Jesse Haines

Jesse Haines played for six teams in the minors between 1914 and 1918 before getting a one-game rookie stint with the Cincinnati Reds in 1918. Haines then spent the next season in the minors before Branch Rickey acquired him. Beginning in 1920, Haines would spend the next 18 years on the mound with the St. Louis Cardinals, winning 210 games while guiding the team to five World Series appearances (1926, 1928, 1930, 1931, and 1934). The Redbirds would win three of those Fall Classics.

Haines's most memorable World Series moment occurred in 1926's Game Seven. After relieving in Game One's loss and shutting out the Yankees in Game Three, Haines had the Cardinals positioned with a lead in Game Seven's finale. But Haines had to leave due to a bleeding blister on his throwing hand with the bases loaded in the seventh inning. His exit from the game led to Grover Alexander's legendary relief appearance that saved the game and won the Series. Always a fierce competitor, his nickname "Pop" was due to the influence he exerted on the Cardinals rising pitching stars. Haines had the credentials to earn their respect during his years with the team. Three times Haines won more than 20 games in a season, and he threw a no-hitter in July of 1924 against the Boston Braves. He is the only player who played on the Cardinals' first five N.L. pennant-winning teams. When he returned to the team for his 18th consecutive season in 1937, he set an N.L. record (since broken) for the longest continuous service with one club. Haines retired after the season at age 44 as the oldest player in the big leagues at the time.

Getty Images

Inducted into the Hall of Fame as a player in 1970 by the Veterans Committee

Position: *Pitcher*

Batted: *Right* **Threw:** *Right*

Height: *6' 0"* **Weight:** *190 lbs.*

Born: *July 22, 1893, in Clayton, OH*

Died: *August 5, 1978, in Dayton, OH*

Buried: *Bethel Cemetery, Phillipsburg, OH*

Debut: *July 20, 1918, with the Cincinnati Reds*

Final game: *September 10, 1937, with the St. Louis Cardinals*

Postseason: *3× World Series Champion (1926, 1931, 1934), 5× N.L. Pennant (1926, 1928, 1930, 1931, 1934)*

Awards & Recognition: *No–hitter on July 17, 1924*

Nickname: *Pop*

Number worn in St. Louis: *Cardinals (18, 16)*

Jesse Haines HOF Pitching Stats – WAR: 32.7

YEAR	TEAM	LG	W	L	ERA	G	CG	SHO	SV	IP	H	HR	BB	SO
1918	CIN	NL	0	0	1.80	1	0	0	0	5	5	0	1	2
1920	STL	NL	13	20	2.98	47	19	4	2	301.2	303	9	80	120
1921	STL	NL	18	12	3.50	37	14	2	0	244.1	261	15	56	84
1922	STL	NL	11	9	3.84	29	11	2	0	183	207	10	45	62
1923	STL	NL	20	13	3.11	37	23	1	0	266	283	7	75	73
1924	STL	NL	8	19	4.41	35	16	1	0	222.2	275	14	66	69
1925	STL	NL	13	14	4.57	29	15	0	0	207	234	11	52	63
1926	STL	NL	13	4	3.25	33	14	3	2	183	186	10	48	46
1927	STL	NL	24	10	2.72	38	25	6	1	300.2	273	11	77	89
1928	STL	NL	20	8	3.18	33	20	1	0	240.1	238	14	72	77
1929	STL	NL	13	10	5.71	28	12	0	0	179.2	230	21	73	59
1930	STL	NL	13	8	4.30	29	14	0	1	182	215	15	54	68
1931	STL	NL	12	3	3.02	19	8	2	0	122.1	134	2	28	27
1932	STL	NL	3	5	4.75	20	4	1	0	85.1	116	4	16	27
1933	STL	NL	9	6	2.50	32	5	0	1	115.1	113	3	37	37
1934	STL	NL	4	4	3.50	37	0	0	1	90	86	6	19	17
1935	STL	NL	6	5	3.59	30	3	0	2	115.1	110	4	28	24
1936	STL	NL	7	5	3.90	25	4	0	1	99.1	110	4	21	19
1937	STL	NL	3	3	4.52	16	2	0	0	65.2	81	5	23	18
Career Totals			210	158	3.64	555	209	23	11	3208.2	3460	165	871	981
STL (18 yrs)		NL	210	158	3.64	554	209	23	11	3203.2	3455	165	870	979

Getty Images

Jake Beckley

Even though his last four years in the majors were with the Cardinals, Jake Beckley is a Hall of Famer little known to St. Louis baseball fans. He had a 19-year N.L. career that began in 1888 and an additional year in the ill-fated Players League in 1890. It was a career without a World Series appearance.

So, who was this unknown first baseman from Hannibal, Missouri? Only Hall of Famer Eddie Murray played more games (2,413) at first base than Beckley (2,383). His Cooperstown plaque describes him as a "famed National League Slugger" and highlights records he held in the majors at the time of his induction at "first base: for chances accepted 25,000 [actually 25,024] most putouts 23,696 [revised to 23,755]." The plaque doesn't mention that "Old Eagle Eye," was one of the game's best contact hitters and retired as the all-time career leader in triples (244), exceeded later by Hall of Famers Sam Crawford, Ty Cobb, and Honus Wagner. One of Beckley's most memorable games came on September 26, 1897, playing for the Cincinnati Reds. He hit three home runs that day against the St. Louis Browns (renamed Cardinals in 1900).

The Cardinals were a last-place team when Beckley arrived from the Reds before the 1904 season. Despite hitting .325 in his first season in St. Louis, he wasn't able to lift the club into contention. They finished fifth, sixth, seventh, and then eighth in his four seasons in St. Louis. Injuries plagued his final two years, so much so that he left the game in 1906 and became an N.L. umpire so he could heal before the following season. His comeback was short-lived, and he retired in June 1907. Despite his accomplishments as one of the N.L. best sluggers, he did not live to enjoy his induction into the Hall of Fame, having passed away 53 years earlier.

Wikimedia Commons

Inducted into the Hall of Fame as a player in 1971 by the Veterans Committee

Position: *First Base*

Batted: *Left* **Threw:** *Left*

Height: *5' 10"* **Weight:** *200 lbs.*

Born: *August 4, 1867, in Hannibal, MO*

Died: *June 25, 1918, in Kansas City, MO*

Buried: *Riverside Cemetery, Hannibal, MO*

Debut: *June 20, 1888, for the Pittsburgh Alleghenys*

Final game: *June 15, 1907, with the St. Louis Cardinals*

Postseason: *N/A*

Awards & Recognition: *5× Top Ten N.L. Batting (1891, 1900, 1902–1904)*

Nickname: *Eagle Eye*

Number worn in St. Louis: *Played prior to numbers being worn*

Jake Beckley – HOF Playing Stats – WAR: 61.2, Slash Line: .308 / .361 / .436

YEAR	TEAM	LG	G	AB	R	H	2B	3B	HR	RBI	SB	BB	SO	BA
1888	PIT	NL	71	283	35	97	15	3	0	27	20	7	22	.343
1889	PIT	NL	123	522	91	157	24	10	9	97	11	29	29	.301
1890	PBB	PL	124	529	110	171	38	22	9	123	18	42	33	.323
1891	PIT	NL	133	554	94	162	20	19	4	73	13	44	46	.292
1892	PIT	NL	151	614	102	145	21	19	10	96	30	31	44	.236
1893	PIT	NL	131	542	108	164	32	19	5	106	15	54	26	.303
1894	PIT	NL	132	537	123	185	36	19	7	122	21	43	16	.345
1895	PIT	NL	130	534	104	175	31	19	5	111	20	24	20	.328
1896	PIT	NL	59	217	44	55	7	5	3	32	8	22	28	.253
1896	NYG	NL	46	182	37	55	8	4	6	38	11	9	7	.302
1897	NYG	NL	17	68	8	17	2	3	1	11	2	2	2	.250
1897	CIN	NL	97	365	76	126	17	9	7	76	23	18	12	.345
1898	CIN	NL	118	459	86	135	20	12	4	72	6	28	27	.294
1899	CIN	NL	135	517	87	172	27	16	3	99	20	40	21	.333
1900	CIN	NL	141	558	98	190	26	10	2	94	23	40	18	.341
1901	CIN	NL	140	580	78	178	36	13	3	79	4	28	37	.307
1902	CIN	NL	129	531	82	175	23	7	5	69	15	34	29	.330
1903	CIN	NL	120	459	85	150	29	10	2	81	23	42	13	.327
1904	**STL**	**NL**	**142**	**551**	**72**	**179**	**22**	**9**	**1**	**67**	**17**	**35**	**31**	**.325**
1905	**STL**	**NL**	**134**	**514**	**48**	**147**	**20**	**10**	**1**	**57**	**12**	**30**	**41**	**.286**
1906	**STL**	**NL**	**87**	**320**	**29**	**79**	**16**	**6**	**0**	**44**	**3**	**13**	**19**	**.247**
1907	**STL**	**NL**	**32**	**115**	**6**	**24**	**3**	**0**	**0**	**7**	**0**	**1**	**5**	**.209**
Career Totals			**2392**	**9551**	**1603**	**2938**	**473**	**244**	**87**	**1581**	**315**	**616**	**526**	**.308**
STL (4 Yrs)		**NL**	**395**	**1500**	**155**	**429**	**61**	**25**	**2**	**175**	**32**	**79**	**96**	**.286**

Library of Congress

Chick Hafey

Charles Hafey, better known as "Chick," is the answer to the trivia question: Who got the first hit in baseball's inaugural All-Star Game in 1933? Hitting is what Hafey did both in that game and throughout his career. After hitting .329 in 1927, the rifle-armed Cardinal leftfielder tallied five straight seasons batting over .330. In July 1929, Hafey tied an N.L. record with 10 hits in 10 consecutive at-bats. Two years later, he led the NL with a .349 average. His winning margin was slim: .00028 over the Giants' Bill Terry, and .00072 over teammate Jim Bottomley. And he did all that with eyesight issues that left baseball historians wondering just how much better he could have been. Hafey's SABR biography quotes the great judge of baseball talent, Branch Rickey, who believed "that if Hafey had been blessed with normal eyesight and good health, he might have been the best right-handed hitter baseball had ever known." That's quite a compliment from the man who mentored the career of a player widely recognized as greatest right-handed hitter of all time—Rogers Hornsby.

Throughout his career Hafey was the most prominent player of his era to wear eyeglasses. A Cardinals utility player from the early 1920s, George Toporcer, was the first to don specs in the field, and Reggie Jackson is the only other Hall of Famer to wear glasses throughout his career.

Hafey became the initial poster boy for Branch Rickey's farm systems through his contributions to the Cardinals' first four World Series appearances between 1926 and 1931. In the end it was Rickey's continuous bickering with players over salary that sent Hafey to Cincinnati to play out the last five years of his career. There's no doubt about Hafey's talent both at the plate and in the field. The question has always been how great he could have been with better eyesight.

Inducted into the Hall of Fame as a player in 1971 by the Veterans Committee

Position: *Outfield*

Batted: *Right* **Threw:** *Right*

Height: *6' 0"* **Weight:** *185 lbs.*

Born: *February 12, 1903, in Berkeley, CA*

Died: *July 2, 1973, in Calistoga, CA*

Buried: *Holy Cross Catholic Cemetery, St. Helena, CA*

Debut: *August 28, 1924, with the St. Louis Cardinals*

Final game: *September 20, 1935, with the Cincinnati Reds*

Postseason: *2× World Series Champion (1926, 1931) 4× N.L. Pennant (1926, 1928, 1930, 1931)*

Awards & Recognition: *All-Star (1931), N.L. Batting Leader (1931)*

Nickname: *Chick*

Number worn in St. Louis: *Played prior to numbers being worn*

Chick Hafey – HOF Playing Stats – WAR: 31.3, Slash Line: .317 / .372 / .526

SEASON	TEAM	LG	G	AB	R	H	2B	3B	HR	RBI	SB	BB	SO	BA
1924	STL	NL	24	91	10	23	5	2	2	22	1	4	8	.253
1925	STL	NL	93	358	36	108	25	2	5	57	3	10	29	.302
1926	STL	NL	78	225	30	61	19	2	4	38	2	11	36	.271
1927	STL	NL	103	346	62	114	26	5	18	63	12	36	41	.329
1928	STL	NL	138	520	101	175	46	6	27	111	8	40	53	.337
1929	STL	NL	134	517	101	175	47	9	29	125	7	45	42	.338
1930	STL	NL	120	446	108	150	39	12	26	107	12	46	51	.336
1931	STL	NL	122	450	94	157	35	8	16	95	11	39	43	.349
1932	CIN	NL	83	253	34	87	19	3	2	36	4	22	20	.344
1933	CIN	NL	144	568	77	172	34	6	7	62	3	40	44	.303
1934	CIN	NL	140	535	75	157	29	6	18	67	4	52	63	.293
1935	CIN	NL	15	59	10	20	6	1	1	9	1	4	5	.339
1937	CIN	NL	89	257	39	67	11	5	9	41	2	23	42	.261
Career Totals			1283	4625	777	1466	341	67	164	833	70	372	477	.317
STL (8 Yrs)		NL	812	2953	542	963	242	46	127	618	56	231	303	.326

Getty Images

Jim Bottomley

He was often referred to as "Sunny Jim" due to his disposition, but a more apt nickname for Jim Bottomley would have been "Mr. Clutch." His Hall of Fame plaque describes him as a "superb clutch hitter." The 1928 MVP hit .310 during his 16 years in the big leagues. There was only one season between 1922 and 1931 when Bottomley didn't hit over .300, (1926's .299). For six seasons in a row he had at least 100 RBIs, twice leading the N.L.

By just several thousandths of a decimal point in 1931, Bottomley missed his shot at winning the N.L. batting title in what remains baseball's closest batting race. His .3482 batting average trailed only Bill Terry's .3486 and N.L. champion Chick Hafey's .3489 averages. Bottomley had a record-setting batting performance in September of 1924 in a game against the Brooklyn Dodgers. He came to bat six times and delivered six hits, including two home runs, a double, and three singles that plated 12 runs. That set an MLB record for RBIs in a game that was later tied by another Cardinal, Mark Whiten, in 1993. Ironically, the record Bottomley broke that day was the Dodgers manager and one-time Cardinal Wilbert Robinson's record of 11 RBIs. Historians have wondered why the Dodger manager didn't intentionally walk Bottomley just once to preserve his own record.

Age and injuries led to Bottomley's trade to the Cincinnati Reds in 1933. After three seasons hitting under .300, he was then traded to the St. Louis Browns to play for his former manager Rogers Hornsby. In 1937, Hornsby was fired, and Bottomley became the Brown's interim manager for the season's final 77 games and a last-place finish. Bottomley would not be retained in 1938, and the player whom the New York Times described as wearing his "baseball cap at a jaunty angle" was out of the big leagues.

Inducted into the Hall of Fame as a player in 1974 by the Veterans Committee

Positions: *First Base, Manager*

Batted: *Left* **Threw:** *Left*

Height: *6' 0"* **Weight:** *180 lbs.*

Born: *April 23, 1900, in Oglesby, IL*

Died: *December 11, 1959, in St. Louis, MO*

Buried: *IOOF Community Cemetery, Sullivan, MO*

Debut: *August 18, 1922, with the St. Louis Cardinals*

Final game: *September 16, 1937, with the St. Louis Browns*

Postseason: *2× World Series Champion (1926, 1931) 4× N.L. Pennant (1926, 1928, 1930, 1931)*

Awards & Recognition: *N.L. MVP (1928), N.L. Home Run Leader (1928), 2× N.L. RBI Leader (1926, 1928)*

Nickname: *Sunny Jim*

Numbers worn in St. Louis: *Cardinals (5, 4) Browns (2)*

Jim Bottomley – Career Managerial Stats

YEAR(S)	SEASONS	TEAM	LEAGUE	WON	LOST	W-L%	TIES	GAMES	EJECTIONS	PENNANTS	CHAMPIONSHIPS
1937	1	SLB	AL	21	56	.273	1	78	0	0	0
Career Totals	1			21	56	.273	1	78	0	0	0

Jim Bottomley – HOF Career Playing Stats – WAR: 35.8, Slash Line: .310 / .369 / .500

YEAR(S)	SEASONS	TEAM	LG	G	AB	R	H	2B	3B	HR	RBI	SB	BB	SO	BA
1922 - 1932	11	STL	NL	1392	5314	921	1727	344	119	181	1105	50	509	429	.325
1933 - 1935	3	CIN	NL	394	1504	173	398	75	21	25	210	7	93	92	.265
1936 - 1937	2	SLB	AL	205	653	83	188	46	11	13	107	1	62	70	.288
Career Totals	16			1991	7471	1177	2313	465	151	219	1422	58	664	591	.310

Missouri Historical Society, St. Louis

Roger Connor

How many baseball fans can quickly name baseball's first home run king? They remember when Hank Aaron broke Babe Ruth's career record in 1974. But whose record did Ruth break? Roger Connor was the home run "king" for over a quarter of a century before Ruth topped the leader board in 1921, He played the last four seasons of his 18-year career in St. Louis. When the power-hitting first baseman with the distinguished handlebar moustache retired in 1897, he was baseball's career home run leader with 138 round-trippers. Twenty-seven of those homers were hit as a member of the N.L. St. Louis Browns (later renamed the Cardinals).

Connor broke into the big leagues with the Troy, New York Trojans in 1880, four years after the N.L. was formed. It was a league in transition, with franchises in cities like Buffalo, Providence, Troy, and Worcester. Playing for Troy on September 10, 1881, with two outs in the bottom of the ninth and the Trojans down by three runs, Connors hit what is considered baseball's first recorded grand slam. It was a walk-off home run that scored four runs to win the game.

Always ranked toward the top in every offensive category, Connor spent 10 of his next 12 seasons playing in New York for a team that in 1883 was called the Gothams. Two seasons later they changed their name to the Giants. Legend has it that Connor's towering presence was the inspiration for the name change. In 1894, at the age of 36, Connor was not getting much playing time and was released in June and then picked up by a not-very-good St. Louis team. While Connor would be at the top of the team's offensive stats during his tenure, the St. Louis team would be at the bottom of the league standings every year.

Library of Congress

Inducted into the Hall of Fame as a player in 1976 by the Veterans Committee

Positions: *First Base, Third Base, Manager*

Batted: *Right* **Threw:** *Right*

Height: *6' 3"* **Weight:** *220 lbs.*

Born: *July 1, 1857, in Waterbury, CT*

Died: *January 4, 1931, in Waterbury, CT*

Buried: *Old St. Joseph Cemetery, Waterbury, CT*

Debut: *May 1, 1880, with the Troy Trojans*

Final game: *May 18, 1897, with the St. Louis Browns (N.L.)*

Postseason: *2× N.L. Champion (1888, 1889)*

Awards & Recognition: *N.L. Batting Leader (1885), N.L. RBI Leader (1889)*

Number worn in St. Louis: *Played prior to numbers being worn*

Roger Connor – Career Managerial Stats

YEAR(S)	SEASONS	TEAM	LEAGUE	WON	LOST	W-L%	TIES	GAMES	EJECTIONS	PENNANTS	CHAMPIONSHIPS
1896	1	STL	NL	8	37	.178	1	46	0	0	0
Career Totals	1			8	37	.178	1	46	0	0	0

Roger Connor – HOF Career Playing Stats – WAR: 84.3, Slash Line: .316 / .397 / .486

YEAR(S)	SEASONS	TEAM	LG	G	AB	R	H	2B	3B	HR	RBI	SB	BB	SO	BA
1880 - 1882	3	TRO	NL	249	1056	173	335	57	32	9	120		41	61	.317
1883 - 1889, 1891, 1893 - 1894	10	NYG	NL	1120	4346	946	1388	242	131	76	786	161	578	276	.319
1890	1	NYI	PL	123	484	133	169	24	15	14	103	22	88	32	.349
1892	1	PHI	NL	155	564	123	166	37	11	12	73	22	116	39	.294
1894 - 1897	4	STL	NL	351	1347	245	409	81	44	27	241	39	179	47	.304
Career Totals	18			1998	7797	1620	2467	441	233	138	1323	244	1002	455	.316

Library of Congress

Bob Gibson

In the nearly 150 years of major league baseball, there have been only a handful of instances where the rules of the game were changed due to a player's performance. In 1968's "year of the pitcher," no one was better than Bob Gibson. His 22–9 record paired with a 1.12 ERA led to the "Gibson Rule," when Major League Baseball reduced the height of the pitcher's mound by five inches, lowering it from 15 inches to 10 inches high due to the Redbird pitcher's dominating season. Gibson's 1968 ERA is the lowest in modern MLB history. That year Gibson started 34 games and completed 28 of them with 13 shutouts. During the months of June and July he never lost a game, earning eight of his 12 wins by shutout. He would win the N.L. MVP and Cy Young Awards for his complete domination from the mound.

But Gibson was not just a one-season wonder. For 17 seasons Gibson was one of the most dominating and intimidating pitchers in the history of the game. And he did it all as a St. Louis Cardinal. How good was the man they called "Gibby?" His Hall of Fame plaque is a testament to greatness: "Five time 20-game winner. His 3,117 strikeouts made him only the second pitcher to reach 3,000." "In 1962 he struck out more than 200 batters for the first time, a feat he would accomplish eight more times. In two of the three World Series in which Gibson pitched he was selected the Series MVP. In his three Fall Classics he won seven consecutive games while throwing eight complete games. In Game One of the 1968 Series Gibson bested Sandy Koufax's record of 15 strikeouts in a Series game by striking out 17 Detroit Tigers on his way to breaking his own 1964 record (31) of most strikeouts in a Series with 35.

Inducted into the Hall of Fame as a player in 1981 (first ballot) by the BBWAA

Position: *Pitcher*

Batted: *Right* **Threw:** *Right*

Height: *6′ 1″* **Weight:** *189 lbs.*

Born: *November 9, 1936, in Omaha, NE*

Died: *October 2, 2020, in Omaha, NE*

Buried: *Evergreen Memorial Park Cemetery, Omaha, NE*

Debut: *April 15, 1959, for the St. Louis Cardinals*

Final game: *September 3, 1975, for the St. Louis Cardinals*

Postseason: *2× World Series Champion (1964, 1967), 3x N.L. Pennant (1964, 1967, 1968)*

Awards & Recognition: *9× All-Star (1962, 1962 (2nd), 1965–1970, 1972), N.L. MVP (1968), 2× Cy Young Award (1968, 1970), 9× Gold Glove Award (1965–1973), N.L. Wins Leader (1970), MLB ERA Leader (1968), N.L. Strikeout Leader (1968), No-hitter (August 14, 1971), MLB All–Century Team*

Nicknames: *Gibby, Hoot*

Number worn in St. Louis: *Cardinals (58, 31, 45—Retired)*

Bob Gibson – HOF Pitching Stats – WAR: 89.2

YEAR	TM	LG	W	L	ERA	G	CG	SHO	SV	IP	H	HR	BB	SO
1959	STL	NL	3	5	3.33	13	2	1	0	75.2	77	4	39	48
1960	STL	NL	3	6	5.61	27	2	0	0	86.2	97	7	48	69
1961	STL	NL	13	12	3.24	35	10	2	1	211.1	186	13	119	166
1962	STL	NL	15	13	2.85	32	15	5	1	233.2	174	15	95	208
1963	STL	NL	18	9	3.39	36	14	2	0	254.2	224	19	96	204
1964	STL	NL	19	12	3.01	40	17	2	1	287.1	250	25	86	245
1965	STL	NL	20	12	3.07	38	20	6	1	299	243	34	103	270
1966	STL	NL	21	12	2.44	35	20	5	0	280.1	210	20	78	225
1967	STL	NL	13	7	2.98	24	10	2	0	175.1	151	10	40	147
1968	STL	NL	22	9	1.12	34	28	13	0	304.2	198	11	62	268
1969	STL	NL	20	13	2.18	35	28	4	0	314	251	12	95	269
1970	STL	NL	23	7	3.12	34	23	3	0	294	262	13	88	274
1971	STL	NL	16	13	3.04	31	20	5	0	245.2	215	14	76	185
1972	STL	NL	19	11	2.46	34	23	4	0	278	226	14	88	208
1973	STL	NL	12	10	2.77	25	13	1	0	195	159	12	57	142
1974	STL	NL	11	13	3.83	33	9	1	0	240	236	24	104	129
1975	STL	NL	3	10	5.04	22	1	0	2	109	120	10	62	60
Career Totals		NL	251	174	2.91	528	255	56	6	3884.1	3279	257	1336	3117

Getty Images

Johnny Mize

This power-hitting first baseman was one of baseball's most feared sluggers. Johnny Mize was nicknamed "the Big Cat" due to the "poise in his stance when he was at bat and his ease while in the field." Mize spent the first six years of his 15-year career with the Cardinals. He then split the remainder of his career in New York with the Giants and Yankees.

Mize joined the Cardinals shortly after the heyday of the Gas House Gang and never got to play in the Fall Classic with the Redbirds. He did, however, appear in five consecutive Series (and won five World Championships) with the Yankees beginning in 1949. During the decade of the 1940s, this perennial All-Star was selected to the Midseason Classic in every year except for those he spent in military service (1943–1945). While teammate Joe Medwick won the Triple Crown in 1937, Mize just missed the same honor in 1939. He led the N.L. with a .349 batting mark and 28 home runs. He fell 19 RBIs short of the Triple Crown. The next season he led the N.L. again with 43 home runs—a mark that remained a Cardinals franchise record until Mark McGwire's 70 dingers in 1998. Mize remains the Cardinals' leader for most home runs in a season and RBIs by a left-handed batter.

All told, Mize was a home run champion four times—once as the N.L. leader and three times as the MLB leader. Mize also hit three more homers during the 1952 World Series. He would top the .300 batting mark nine seasons in a row and retired having hit three home runs in a game six times, an MLB record that has since been tied by Sammy Sosa and Mookie Betts. At his retirement, Mize was only the second player to have had 25-home-run seasons in each league.

Wikimedia Commons

Inducted into the Hall of Fame as a player in 1981 by the Veterans Committee

Position: *First Base*

Batted: *Left* **Threw:** *Right*

Height: *6' 2"* **Weight:** *215 lbs.*

Born: *January 7, 1913, in Demorest, GA*

Died: *June 2, 1993, in Demorest, GA*

Buried: *Yonah View Memorial Gardens, Demorest, GA*

Debut: *April 16, 1936, with the St. Louis Cardinals*

Final game: *September 26, 1953, with the New York Yankees*

Postseason: *5× World Series Champion (1949–1953), 5× A.L. Pennant (1949–1953)*

Awards & Recognition: *10× All-Star (1937, 1939–1942, 1946–1949, 1953), N.L. Batting Leader (1939), 4× N.L. Home Run Leader (1939, 1940, 1947, 1948), 3× N.L. RBI Leader (1940, 1942, 1947),*

Nicknames: *The Big Cat, Big Jawn*

Number worn in St. Louis: *Cardinals (10)*

Johnny Mize – HOF Playing Stats – WAR: 70.6, Slash Line: .312 / .397 / .562

SEASON	TEAM	LG	G	AB	R	H	2B	3B	HR	RBI	SB	BB	SO	BA
1936	STL	NL	126	414	76	136	30	8	19	93	1	50	32	.329
1937	STL	NL	145	560	103	204	40	7	25	113	2	56	57	.364
1938	STL	NL	149	531	85	179	34	16	27	102	0	74	47	.337
1939	STL	NL	153	564	104	197	44	14	28	108	0	92	49	.349
1940	STL	NL	155	579	111	182	31	13	43	137	7	82	49	.314
1941	STL	NL	126	473	67	150	39	8	16	100	4	70	45	.317
1942	NYG	NL	142	541	97	165	25	7	26	110	3	60	39	.305
1943	Did not play - Military Service													
1944	Did not play - Military Service													
1945	Did not play - Military Service													
1946	NYG	NL	101	377	70	127	18	3	22	70	3	62	26	.337
1947	NYG	NL	154	586	137	177	26	2	51	138	2	74	42	.302
1948	NYG	NL	152	560	110	162	26	4	40	125	4	94	37	.289
1949	NYG	NL	106	388	59	102	15	0	18	62	1	50	19	.263
1949	NYY	AL	13	23	4	6	1	0	1	2	0	4	2	.261
1950	NYY	AL	90	274	43	76	12	0	25	72	0	29	24	.277
1951	NYY	AL	113	332	37	86	14	1	10	49	1	36	24	.259
1952	NYY	AL	78	137	9	36	9	0	4	29	0	11	15	.263
1953	NYY	AL	81	104	6	26	3	0	4	27	0	12	17	.250
Career Totals			1884	6443	1118	2011	367	83	359	1337	28	856	524	.312
STL (6 Yrs)		NL	854	3121	546	1048	218	66	158	653	14	424	279	.336

Walter Alston

Walter Alston's induction into the Hall of Fame came in recognition of his 23-year career managing the Dodgers in both Brooklyn and Los Angeles. Many Hall of Fame managers spent time playing baseball in the big leagues before leading a team. The same was true for Alston. However, it's a bit of a stretch to call a single game in the majors a "career." That one game (two innings played and one at-bat) came as a St. Louis Cardinal in 1936.

Alston began his professional career in the Cardinals' minor league organization in 1935. After batting .326 that year for the Class C Chiefs of Greenwood, Mississippi, he wound up hitting the exact same mark the next year in Huntington, West Virginia, while hitting 35 home runs and playing third base. That performance earned him a late-September call up to the parent club as insurance in the team's unsuccessful pennant run.

That insurance policy came into play on September 27, 1936. Johnny Mize was ejected in the final game of the season and manager Frankie Frisch sent Alston in to make his major league debut at first base. While the memory of playing in a big-league game may be special, his performance was not so memorable. Alston only had two chances in the field and made an error on one of them. He only walked to the plate one time and struck out on three pitches. Mize would become a staple at first base and Alston would play no more in the majors.

Alston would spend the next 16 years playing and managing in the minor leagues before taking over the helm of the Brooklyn Dodgers in 1954. He remained with the team when they moved to Los Angeles in 1958, retiring after the 1976 season. His teams would win seven pennants and hoist the World Championship flag four times, including Brooklyn's only championship in 1955.

Inducted into the Hall of Fame as a manager in 1983 by the Veterans Committee

Positions: *First Base, Manager*

Batted: *Right* **Threw:** *Right*

Height: *6' 2"* **Weight:** *195 lbs.*

Born: *December 1, 1911, in Venice, OH*

Died: *October 1, 1984, in Oxford, OH*

Buried: *Darrtown Cemetery, Darrtown, OH*

Debut: *September 27, 1936, with the St. Louis Cardinals*

Final game: *September 27, 1936, with the St. Louis Cardinals*

Postseason: *4× World Series Champion (Manager—1955, 1959, 1963, 1965), 7× N.L. Pennant (Manager—1955, 1956, 1959, 1963, 1965, 1966, 1974)*

Awards & Recognition: *9× All-Star Game Manager (1954, 1956, 1957, 1960, 1960 (2nd), 1964, 1966, 1967, 1975)*

Nickname: *Smokey*

Number worn in St. Louis: *Cardinals (21)*

Walter Alston– HOF Career Managerial Stats

YEAR(S)	SEASONS	TEAM	LEAGUE	WON	LOST	W-L%	TIES	GAMES	EJECTIONS	PENNANTS	CHAMPIONSHIPS
1954 - 1957	4	BRO	NL	367	248	.596	1	616	8	2	1
1957 - 1976	19	LAD	NL	1673	1365	.550	4	3042	29	5	3
Career Totals	**23**			**2040**	**1613**	**.558**	**5**	**3658**	**37**	**7**	**4**

Walter Alston – HOF Career Playing Stats – WAR: 0.0, Slash Line: 0.000 / 0.000 / 0.00

YEAR(S)	SEASONS	TEAM	LEAGUE	G	AB	R	H	2B	3B	HR	RBI	SB	BB	SO	BA
1936	1	STL	NL	1	1	0	0	0	0	0	0	0	0	1	.000
Career Totals	1			1	1	0	0	0	0	0	0	0	0	1	.000

Dodgers
Getty Images

Lou Brock

For nearly two decades Lou Brock ran, and he ran all the way into baseball's record books as one of the game's most prolific base-stealers. He led the N.L. in steals every season but one (1970) in the nine seasons from 1966 to 1974, and in six of those seasons he was the major league leader. In 1974 Brock shattered Maury Wills's 1962 mark of 104 steals in a season to claim a new record of 118 steals. In 1977 Brock broke Ty Cobb's career record of 892 stolen bases, a mark that had stood since 1928. When Brock retired in 1979, his 938 stolen bases topped the record books until Ricky Henderson became the new stolen base king in May 1991.

But Lou Brock was much more than a base burglar. He was one of the game's most exciting and dangerous players during the 1960s and 1970s. Lou retired in 1979 as only the 14th player to collect 3,000 hits in the history of the game (3,023) while playing 19 seasons with the Chicago Cubs and the St. Louis Cardinals. His 1964 trade from Chicago to St. Louis for Ernie Broglio and two other players is viewed as one of the game's most lopsided swaps.

With Brock added to a team that already included Curt Flood and Bob Gibson, the trio of stars combined speed, defense, and pitching and won three pennants and two World Championships between 1964 and 1968. While Gibson was overpowering on the mound in those Fall Classics, Brock dominated at the plate and on the basepaths. He batted .391 while slugging .655 in his 21 World Series games, including four home runs and 14 stolen bases. Good to the end, Brock batted .309 in his final season and was selected as baseball's Comeback Player of the Year.

Inducted into the Hall of Fame in as a player in 1985 (first ballot) by the BBWAA

Position: *Left Field*

Batted: *Left* **Threw:** *Left*

Height *5' 11"* **Weight:** *170 lbs.*

Born: *June 18, 1938, in El Dorado, AR*

Died: *September 6, 2020, in St. Charles, MO*

Buried: *Forever Bellerive Cemetery, Creve Coeur, MO*

Debut: *September 19, 1961, with the Chicago Cubs*

Final game: *September 30, 1979, with the St. Louis Cardinals*

Postseason: *2× World Series Champion (1964, 1967), 3x N.L. Pennant (1964, 1967, 1968)*

Awards & Recognition: *6× All-Star (1967, 1971, 1972, 1974, 1975, 1979), 8× Stolen Base Leader (1966–1969, 1971–1974), Roberto Clemente Award Winner (1975)*

Nicknames: *The Franchise, The Rocket*

Number worn in St. Louis: *Cardinals (20)*

Lou Brock – HOF Playing Stats WAR: 45.3, Slash Line: .293 / .343 / .410

SEASON	TEAM	LG	G	AB	R	H	2B	3B	HR	RBI	SB	BB	SO	BA
1961	CHC	NL	4	11	1	1	0	0	0	0	0	1	3	.091
1962	CHC	NL	123	434	73	114	24	7	9	35	16	35	96	.263
1963	CHC	NL	148	547	79	141	19	11	9	37	24	31	122	.258
1964	CHC	NL	52	215	30	54	9	2	2	14	10	13	40	.251
1964	STL	NL	103	419	81	146	21	9	12	44	33	27	87	.348
1965	STL	NL	155	631	107	182	35	8	16	69	63	45	116	.288
1966	STL	NL	156	643	94	183	24	12	15	46	74	31	134	.285
1967	STL	NL	159	689	113	206	32	12	21	76	52	24	109	.299
1968	STL	NL	159	660	92	184	46	14	6	51	62	46	124	.279
1969	STL	NL	157	655	97	195	33	10	12	47	53	50	115	.298
1970	STL	NL	155	664	114	202	29	5	13	57	51	60	99	.304
1971	STL	NL	157	640	126	200	37	7	7	61	64	76	107	.313
1972	STL	NL	153	621	81	193	26	8	3	42	63	47	93	.311
1973	STL	NL	160	650	110	193	29	8	7	63	70	71	112	.297
1974	STL	NL	153	635	105	194	25	7	3	48	118	61	88	.306
1975	STL	NL	136	528	78	163	27	6	3	47	56	38	64	.309
1976	STL	NL	133	498	73	150	24	5	4	67	56	35	75	.301
1977	STL	NL	141	489	69	133	22	6	2	46	35	30	74	.272
1978	STL	NL	92	298	31	66	9	0	0	12	17	17	29	.221
1979	STL	NL	120	405	56	123	15	4	5	38	21	23	43	.304
Career Totals		NL	2616	10332	1610	3023	486	141	149	900	938	761	1730	.293
STL (16 Yrs)		NL	2289	9125	1427	2713	434	121	129	814	888	681	1469	.297

Getty Images

Enos Slaughter

Long before Pete Rose was given the moniker "Charlie Hustle," baseball's true "Mr. Hustle" was Enos Slaughter. Slaughter's hustle became legendary after one "mad dash" in the seventh game of the 1946 World Series. The play was ranked number 10 in the Sporting News's 1999 list of Baseball's Greatest Moments.

In his first five seasons with the Cardinals, Slaughter batted over .300 and was a two-time All-Star. He was also a World Series Champion in 1942 after his Cardinals defeated the Yankees in the Fall Classic. Like many ballplayers, Slaughter was drafted into WWII and missed the next three seasons. When he put the Cardinals uniform back on in 1946, he wasted little time getting back into the game. He hit .300 and led the majors in RBIs with 130 as the Redbirds won their fourth pennant in five years.

In 1946's seven-game Series against the Red Sox, Slaughter batted .320, but he will always be remembered for what he did when he got on base with the game tied in the eighth inning of the Series finale. With Slaughter on first and two outs, Harry Walker lined a hit to center field, and Slaughter was off and running. To the surprise of everyone, including the Red Sox, he ran through the coach's stop sign at third and slid into home beating the throw to deliver what would be the winning run after the Cardinals held the Sox scoreless in the top of the ninth.

Slaughter was named to every All-Star game from 1946 to 1953 before being traded to the Yankees at the start of the 1954 season. In the remaining six years of his career, Slaughter won three pennants and two World Series Championships with the Yankees (1956–1958). A Cardinal to the end, Slaughter was buried in a Cardinals uniform with a bat and ball at his side.

Missouri Historical Society, St. Louis

Inducted into the Hall of Fame as a player in 1985 by the Veterans Committee

Position: *Right Field*

Batted: *Left* **Threw:** *Right*

Height: *5' 9"* **Weight:** *180 lbs.*

Born: *April 27, 1916, in Roxboro, NC*

Died: *August 12, 2002, in Durham, NC*

Buried: *Allensville United Methodist Church Cemetery, Roxboro, NC*

Debut: *April 19, 1938, with the St. Louis Cardinals*

Final game: *September 29, 1959, with the Milwaukee Braves*

Postseason: *4× World Series Champion (1942, 1946, 1956, 1958), 2x N.L. Pennant (1942, 1946), 3x A.L. Pennant (1956, 1957, 1958)*

Awards & Recognition: *10× All-Star (1941, 1942, 1946–1953), N.L. RBI Leader (1946)*

Nickname: *Country*

Number worn in St. Louis: *Cardinals (9–retired)*

Enos Slaughter – HOF Playing Stats – WAR: 57.6, Slash Line: .300 / .382 / .453

SEASON	TEAM	LG	G	AB	R	H	2B	3B	HR	RBI	SB	BB	SO	BA
1938	STL	NL	112	395	59	109	20	10	8	58	1	32	38	.276
1939	STL	NL	149	604	95	193	52	5	12	86	2	44	53	.320
1940	STL	NL	140	516	96	158	25	13	17	73	8	50	35	.306
1941	STL	NL	113	425	71	132	22	9	13	76	4	53	28	.311
1942	STL	NL	152	591	100	188	31	17	13	98	9	88	30	.318
1943-45	Did not play - Military Service													
1946	STL	NL	156	609	100	183	30	8	18	130	9	69	41	.300
1947	STL	NL	147	551	100	162	31	13	10	86	4	59	27	.294
1948	STL	NL	146	549	91	176	27	11	11	90	4	81	29	.321
1949	STL	NL	151	568	92	191	34	13	13	96	3	79	37	.336
1950	STL	NL	148	556	82	161	26	7	10	101	3	66	33	.290
1951	STL	NL	123	409	48	115	17	8	4	64	7	67	25	.281
1952	STL	NL	140	510	73	153	17	12	11	101	6	70	25	.300
1953	STL	NL	143	492	64	143	34	9	6	89	4	80	28	.291
1954	NYY	AL	69	125	19	31	4	2	1	19	0	28	8	.248
1955	NYY	AL	10	9	1	1	0	0	0	1	0	1	1	.111
1955	KCA	AL	108	267	49	86	12	4	5	34	2	40	17	.322
1956	KCA	AL	91	223	37	62	14	3	2	23	1	29	20	.278
1956	NYY	AL	24	83	15	24	4	2	0	4	1	5	6	.289
1957	NYY	AL	96	209	24	53	7	1	5	34	0	40	19	.254
1958	NYY	AL	77	138	21	42	4	1	4	19	2	21	16	.304
1959	NYY	AL	74	99	10	17	2	0	6	21	1	13	19	.172
1959	MLN	NL	11	18	0	3	0	0	0	1	0	3	3	.167
Career Totals			2380	7946	1247	2383	413	148	169	1304	71	1018	538	.300
STL (13 Yrs)		NL	1820	6775	1071	2064	366	135	146	1148	64	838	429	.305

Getty Images

Hoyt Wilhelm

Hoyt Wilhelm was not some young, strapping, hard-throwing pitcher when he reached the majors in 1952. In fact, he wasn't young at all. He was 29 years old. The wounded WWII veteran had toiled for seven years in the minors before getting called up. When he finally quit pitching in 1972, he was weeks shy of his 50th birthday.

What led to this longevity in the game? Wilhelm was the master of a freak pitch—the knuckleball—and he threw it better than any of his predecessors. His greatness came not as a starting pitcher, even though his stats as a starter were better than most. His game-changing evolution as the master of relief led to the relief specialists found in today's game, and it set the stage for Wilhelm to be the first relief pitcher inducted into the Hall of Fame in 1985. Wilhelm finished his first season with the best winning percentage in the game thanks to a 15–3 record. He led the N.L. in ERA while leading the majors in games pitched, and he did it all without starting a single game. It was the first and only ERA title to go to a relief pitcher.

At age 35 in his seventh season in 1958, Wilhelm finally got to start a game—a trend that continued the next two seasons before he went back to pitching exclusively in relief. In desperate need of a first baseman, the Giants sent Wilhelm to the Cardinals in 1957 for Whitey Lockman. The Redbirds were in a tight race, but Wilhelm didn't help the cause (4.25 ERA) and was released in September before the Cardinals fell out of the pennant race and eventually finished in second place. Wilhelm stayed in the game for seven different teams over the next 15 seasons. Most were with the the White Sox during the mid-1960s, when Wilhelm went 41–33 with 99 saves and a 1.92 ERA in 361 games, all of which came after his 40th birthday.

Wikimedia Commons

Inducted into the Hall of Fame as a player in 1985 by the BBWAA

Position: *Pitcher*

Batted: *Right* **Threw:** *Right*

Height: *6' 0"* **Weight:** *190 lbs.*

Born: *July 26, 1922, in Huntersville, NC*

Died: *August 23, 2002, in Sarasota, FL*

Buried: *Palms Memorial Park, Sarasota, FL*

Debut: *April 18, 1952, with the New York Giants*

Final game: *July 10, 1972, with the Los Angeles Dodgers*

Postseason: *World Series Champion (1954), N.L. Pennant (1954)*

Awards & Recognition: *8× All-Star (1953, 1959, 1959 (2nd), 1961, 1961 (2nd), 1962, 1962 (2nd),1970), 2× ERA Leader (1952, 1959), No-hitter (September 20, 1958)*

Nickname: *Old Sarge*

Number worn in St. Louis: *Cardinals (25)*

Hoyt Wilhelm – HOF Career Playing Stats – WAR: 46.8

YEAR(S)	SEASONS	TEAM	LEAGUE	W	L	ERA	G	CG	SHO	SV	IP	H	HR	BB	SO
1952 - 1956	5	NYG	NL	42	25	2.98	319	0	0	41	608	532	47	269	385
1957	**1**	**STL**	**NL**	**1**	**4**	**4.25**	**40**	**0**	**0**	**11**	**55**	**52**	**7**	**21**	**29**
1957 - 1958	2	CLE	AL	3	7	2.49	32	1	0	6	94	72	5	36	57
1958 - 1962	5	BAL	AL	43	39	2.42	185	19	5	40	616.1	481	38	201	458
1963 - 1968	6	CHW	AL	41	33	1.92	361	0	0	99	675.2	465	38	167	521
1969	1	CAL	AL	5	7	2.47	44	0	0	10	65.2	45	4	18	53
1969 - 1970, 1971	3	ATL	NL	8	4	3.10	61	0	0	17	93	80	9	44	82
1970	1	CHC	NL	0	1	9.82	3	0	0	0	3.2	4	1	3	1
1971 - 1972	2	LAD	NL	0	2	3.14	25	0	0	4	43	26	1	19	24
Career Totals	**21**			**143**	**122**	**2.52**	**1070**	**20**	**5**	**228**	**2254.1**	**1757**	**150**	**778**	**1610**

Getty Images

Red Schoendienst

Red Schoendienst grew up across the Mississippi River from St. Louis loving the Redbirds. He would go on to have a tenure of over 60 years with the club. His Hall of Fame plaque described him as a “sleek, far-ranging second baseman” who “led the N.L. in fielding and hit .300 or better seven times.” His .9934 fielding percentage at second base in 1956 set a N.L. record that stood for 30 years until Ryne Sandberg exceeded it in 1986. Red made his big-league debut in 1945 not in the infield but rather in left field wearing uniform number 6. Red would be the last Cardinal to wear that number before Stan Musial returned from the Navy in 1946 and wore it once again until his retirement in 1963. In that rookie season Red showed another of his many talents by leading the N.L. in stolen bases.

Red became the regular second baseman in 1946 and made the first of his 10 All-Star appearances while winning his first World Championship when the Cardinals defeated the Boston Red Sox. In 1950 he handled 320 consecutive fielding chances without an error and became an All-Star game hero with a game winning homer in the 14th inning of the Midseason Classic’s first extra-inning game. Red had become a steady cog in the Cardinals’ lineup when he was traded to the Giants for Alvin Dark in 1956. A year later Red was traded to the Milwaukee Braves, where he led the majors with 200 hits and made the All-Star team as the Braves won the first of their two consecutive World Series appearances.

In 1961 Red rejoined the Cardinals as a player-coach for the final three years of his on-field career. In 1964 Red moved into the dugout as a full-time coach before ascending the next year to become the team’s manager for the next 12 seasons. Twice he guided his team to pennants (1967, 1968) and he won the World Series in 1967. From the field to the dugout, Red surely did it all.

State Historical Society of Missouri

Inducted into the Hall of Fame as a player in 1989 by the Veterans Committee

Positions: *Second Base, Left Field, Manager*

Batted: *Both* **Threw:** *Right*

Height: *6′ 0″* **Weight:** *170 lbs.*

Born: *February 2, 1923, in Germantown, IL*

Died: *June 6, 2018, in Town and Country, MO*

Buried: *Resurrection Cemetery, St. Louis, MO*

Debut: *April 17, 1945, with the St. Louis Cardinals*

Final game: *July 7, 1963, with the St. Louis Cardinals*

Postseason: *3× World Series Champion (Player—1946, 1957; Manager—1967), 5× N.L. Pennant (Player—1946, 1957, 1958, Manager—1967, 1968)*

Awards & Recognition: *10× All-Star (1946, 1948–1955, 1957), N.L. Stolen Base Leader (1945)*

Nickname: *Red*

Number worn in St. Louis: *Cardinals (6, 2—retired)*

Red Schoendienst – HOF Career Managerial Stats

YEAR(S)	SEASONS	TEAM	LEAGUE	WON	LOST	W-L%	TIES	GAMES	EJECTIONS	PENNANTS	CHAMPIONSHIPS
1965 - 1976, 1980, 1990	14	STL	NL	1041	955	.522	3	1999	12	2	1

Red Schoendienst – Career Playing Stats – WAR: 44.8, Slash Line: .289 / .337 / .387

YEAR(S)	SEASONS	TEAM	LEAGUE	G	AB	R	H	2B	3B	HR	RBI	SB	BB	SO	BA
1945 - 1956, 1961 - 1963	15	STL	NL	1795	6841	1025	1980	352	65	65	651	80	497	287	.289
1956 - 1957	2	NYG	NI	149	588	74	177	20	7	11	47	3	38	18	.301
1957 - 1960	4	MLN	NL	272	1050	124	292	55	6	8	75	6	71	41	.278
Career Totals	**19**			**2216**	**8479**	**1223**	**2449**	**427**	**78**	**84**	**773**	**89**	**606**	**346**	**.289**

Missouri Historical Society, St. Louis

★ ★

Steve Carlton

Steve Carlton spent 24 years as one of baseball's greatest pitchers, winning 329 games. He won more than 20 games six times. Carlton helped the Cardinals win a World Championship in 1967 and an N.L. pennant in 1968. His dominance on the mound was demonstrated in September 1969, when he set a major league record by striking out 19 batters in a nine-inning game against the Mets. Carlton's impressive numbers and his independent nature led to annual demands for a higher salary than he was offered. A $5,000 salary gap could not be closed in 1972, when the Cardinals offered $60,000 and Carlton wanted $65,000. Redbird owner August Busch refused to budge and shipped Carlton off to the last-place Philadelphia Phillies in exchange for pitcher Rick Wise.

Carlton quickly showed Busch his worth. In his first season in Philadelphia Carlton led the N.L. in wins, ERA, innings pitched, and strikeouts. While the Phillies were bad, Carlton was great. He won 27 games, or 46 percent of the wins for the 59–97 last-place Phillies in 1972. Carlton won the first of his four Cy Young Awards that season. In his 15 seasons with the Phillies Carlton chalked up 241 wins. He led the N.L. in wins four times while adding seven more All-Star appearances to the three earned in St. Louis. In 1983, Carlton became the 16th pitcher in baseball to win 300 games. In August 1986, Carlton joined Nolan Ryan as the only two pitchers in MLB history to date to record four thousand strikeouts. He would strike out another 136 more batters before retiring two years later at age 43.

How many more pennants would the Cardinals have won if ownership had paid that $5,000? In each of the 1973 and 1974 seasons the Cardinals finished second, 1-1/2 games out of first place. Surely Carlton would have made a difference in those two years and many more.

Inducted into the Hall of Fame as a player in 1994 (first ballot) by the BBWAA

Position: *Pitcher*

Batted: *Left* **Threw:** *Left*

Height: *6' 4"* **Weight:** *210 lbs.*

Born: *December 22, 1944, in Miami, FL*

Debut: *April 12, 1965, with the St. Louis Cardinals*

Final game: *April 23, 1988, with the Minnesota Twins*

Postseason: *2× World Series Champion (1967, 1980), 4× N.L. Pennant (1967, 1968, 1980, 1983)*

Awards & Recognition: *10× All-Star (1968, 1969, 1971, 1972, 1974, 1977, 1979–1982), 4× N.L. Cy Young Award (1972, 1977, 1980, 1982), Pitching Triple Crown (1972), Gold Glove Award (1981), 4× N.L. Wins Leader (1972, 1977, 1980, 1982), N.L. ERA Leader (1972), 5× N.L. Strikeout Leader (1972, 1974, 1980, 1982, 1983)*

Nickname: *Lefty*

Number worn in St. Louis: *Cardinals (32)*

Steve Carlton – HOF Career Playing Stats – WAR: 90.2

YEAR(S)	SEASONS	TEAM	LEAGUE	W	L	ERA	G	CG	SHO	SV	IP	H	HR	BB	SO
1965 - 1971	**7**	**STL**	**NL**	**77**	**62**	**3.10**	**190**	**66**	**16**	**1**	**1265.1**	**1169**	**89**	**449**	**951**
1972 - 1986	15	PHI	NL	241	161	3.09	499	185	39	0	3697.1	3224	286	1252	3031
1986	1	SFG	NL	1	3	5.10	6	0	0	0	30.0	36	4	16	18
1986	1	CHW	AL	4	3	3.69	10	0	0	0	63.1	58	6	25	40
1987	1	CLE	AL	5	9	5.37	23	3	0	1	109.0	111	17	63	71
1987 - 1988	2	MIN	AL	1	6	8.54	13	0	0	0	52.2	74	12	28	25
Career Totals	**24**			**329**	**244**	**3.11**	**741**	**254**	**55**	**2**	**5217.2**	**4672**	**414**	**1833**	**4136**

Getty Images

Leo Durocher

Leo Durocher was the fiery and controversial skipper of four big league teams over a 24-year managerial career. While at the helm, he won three pennants and a World Series. His nickname, "the Lip," was indicative of his combative nature. But before he became a dugout leader, Durocher spent 17 years on the field as a good-glove, mediocre-hitting shortstop.

His playing days began playing alongside Babe Ruth and Lou Gehrig in 1928, a season that ended with the Yankees defeating the Cardinals in the World Series. After a stint with the Reds, Durocher spent five seasons in St. Louis during the heyday of the Gas House Gang. Durocher's scrappy and cantankerous nature seemed a perfect fit for the rough-and-tumble Cardinals. His aggressive ways led to his becoming the captain of the 1934 World Series Champions. Durocher's career-best season came in 1936, when he was rewarded with the first of his three All-Star appearances. But Leo "the Lip's" schtick wore thin on Cardinals player–manager Frankie Frisch, and Durocher was shipped off to Brooklyn after the 1937 season.

In his second season with the Dodgers, Durocher became the team's player–manager, and two years later the Dodgers won the 1941 NL pennant. In 1946 the Dodgers were tied for first with the Cardinals at the end of the season but lost to the Redbirds in the subsequent playoff. The next season Durocher was suspended from baseball for associating with known gamblers, and his comeback in 1948 didn't begin well. With the Dodgers off to a bad start, Durocher was sent to the Giants to become their new manager. He would lead the team to pennants in 1951 and 1954—the latter a World Championship. After a decade away from managing, Durocher took the helm of the Chicago Cubs in 1966 before finishing with the Astros in 1973 as baseball's fifth-winningest manager and second only to John McGraw in the National League.

Inducted into the Hall of Fame as a manager in 1994 by the Veterans Committee

Positions: *Shortstop, Second Base, Manager*

Batted: *Right* **Threw:** *Right*

Height: *5' 10"* **Weight:** *160 lbs.*

Born: *July 27, 1905, in West Springfield, MA*

Died: *October 7, 1991, in Palm Springs, CA*

Buried: *Forest Lawn-Hollywood Hills, Los Angeles, CA*

Debut: *October 2, 1925, with the New York Yankees*

Final game: *April 18, 1945, with the Brooklyn Dodgers*

Postseason: *3× World Series Champion (Player—1928, 1934, Manager—1954), 1x A.L. Pennant (Player–1928), 4x N.L. Pennant (1934, 1941, 1951, 1954)*

Awards & Recognition: *3× All-Star (1936, 1938, 1940)*

Nickname: *The Lip*

Number worn in St. Louis: *Cardinals (2)*

Leo Durocher – HOF Career Managerial Stats

YEAR(S)	SEASONS	TEAM	LEAGUE	WON	LOST	W-L%	TIES	GAMES	EJECTIONS	PENNANTS	CHAMPIONSHIPS
1939 - 1946, 1948	9 years	BLN	NL	738	565	.566	15	1318	44	1	0
1948 - 1955	8 years	NYG	NL	637	523	.549	3	1163	34	2	1
1966 - 1972	7 years	CHC	NL	535	526	.504	4	1065	20	0	0
1972 - 1973	2 years	HOU	NL	98	95	.508	0	193	2	0	0
Career Totals	**24 years**		**NL**	**2008**	**1709**	**.540**	**22**	**3739**	**100**	**3**	**1**

Leo Durocher– Career Playing Stats – WAR: 4.3, Slash Line: .247 / .299 / .320

YEAR(S)	SEASONS	TEAM	LEAGUE	G	AB	R	H	2B	3B	HR	RBI	SB	BB	SO	BA
1925, 1928 - 1929	3	NYY	AL	210	638	100	164	12	11	0	63	4	56	85	.257
1930 - 1933	4	CIN	NL	399	1223	106	278	49	13	6	97	3	78	122	.227
1933 - 1937	**5**	**STL**	**NL**	**683**	**2395**	**272**	**611**	**100**	**20**	**15**	**294**	**18**	**155**	**201**	**.255**
1938 - 1941, 1943, 1945	6	BRO	NL	345	1094	97	267	49	12	3	113	6	88	72	.244
Career Totals	**17**			**1637**	**5350**	**575**	**1320**	**210**	**56**	**24**	**567**	**31**	**377**	**480**	**.247**

Getty Images

Vic Willis

In just 13 big league seasons pitcher Vic Willis won 249 games. That averages to just over 19 wins a season. Eight times he won 20 or more games in a season during a career that included 50 shutouts and a 2.63 ERA. He was a durable starter, completing 388 (82%) of his career 471 starts.

Willis pitched his final season with the N.L. St. Louis Cardinals in 1910. His career started with the N.L. Boston Beaneaters (later Braves) in 1898. Teaming with future Hall of Famer Kid Nichols, Willis had an impressive 25–13 record as a rookie, helping the team win its fifth N.L. pennant since 1891. Even though Willis's 27–8 mark the following year—which included a no-hitter—was even better, his team finished in second place and would never hoist another pennant during his tenure in Boston. In 1902 Willis set the modern-day (since 1901) record for complete games pitched in an N.L. season by completing 45 of the 46 games he started. That same year, Willis pitched 410 innings, the second-highest total in modern N.L. history. Three years later he lost 29 games in 1905 to claim the modern-day record for most losses in a major league season.

After eight years and 151 wins Willis was traded in 1906 to the Pittsburgh Pirates, where his four straight years of 20-plus wins would eventually lead the team to a 1909 World Series victory over Ty Cobb's Detroit Tigers. Despite winning 22 games in 1909, Willis was waived due to "disciplinary issues" with the Pirates Manager Fred Clarke. St. Louis claimed Willis off waivers hoping to improve their team's performance, but Willis's performance did not meet expectations. He was released just before the end of the 1910 season with a 9–12 record—his final season in the big leagues.

Library of Congress

Inducted into the Hall of Fame as a player in 1995 by the Veterans Committee

Position: *Pitcher*

Batted: *Right* **Threw:** *Right*

Height: *6' 2"* **Weight:** *185 lbs.*

Born: *April 12, 1876, in Cecil County, MD*

Died: *August 3, 1947, in Elkton, MD*

Buried: *St. John Cemetery, Newark, DE*

Debut: *April 20, 1898, with the Boston Beaneaters*

Final game: *September 5, 1910, for the St. Louis Cardinals*

Postseason: *World Series Champion (1909), 2x N.L. Champion (1898, 1909)*

Awards & Recognition: *No-hitter (August 7, 1899)*

Number worn in St. Louis: *Played prior to numbers being worn*

Vic Willis – HOF Pitching Stats – WAR: 63.2

YEAR	TEAM	LEAGUE	W	L	ERA	G	CG	SHO	SV	IP	H	HR	BB	SO
1898	BSN	NL	25	13	2.84	41	29	1	0	311	264	5	148	160
1899	BSN	NL	27	8	2.50	41	35	5	2	342.2	277	6	117	120
1900	BSN	NL	10	17	4.19	32	22	2	0	236	258	11	106	53
1901	BSN	NL	20	17	2.36	38	33	6	0	305.1	262	6	78	133
1902	BSN	NL	27	20	2.20	51	45	4	3	410	372	6	101	225
1903	BSN	NL	12	18	2.98	33	29	2	0	278	256	3	88	125
1904	BSN	NL	18	25	2.85	43	39	2	0	350	357	7	109	196
1905	BSN	NL	12	29	3.21	41	36	4	0	342	340	7	107	149
1906	PIT	NL	23	13	1.73	41	32	6	1	322	295	0	76	124
1907	PIT	NL	21	11	2.34	39	27	6	1	292.2	234	4	69	107
1908	PIT	NL	23	11	2.07	41	25	7	0	304.2	239	2	69	97
1909	PIT	NL	22	11	2.24	39	24	4	1	289.2	243	3	83	95
1910	**STL**	**NL**	**9**	**12**	**3.35**	**33**	**12**	**1**	**3**	**212**	**224**	**6**	**61**	**67**
Career Totals		**NL**	**249**	**205**	**2.63**	**513**	**388**	**50**	**11**	**3996**	**3621**	**66**	**1212**	**1651**
STL (1 yr)		**NL**	**9**	**12**	**3.35**	**33**	**12**	**1**	**3**	**212**	**224**	**6**	**61**	**67**

Library of Congress

Orlando Cepeda

Orlando Cepeda's 1958 rookie season with the San Francisco Giants was a preview of what was to come. He was the unanimous selection as the N.L. Rookie of the Year. A decade later with the Cardinals, he was the unanimous selection as the N.L. Most Valuable Player. In between these awards, Cepeda became an 11-time All-Star.

Cepeda almost won the MVP a decade earlier in 1961. Finishing second to Frank Robinson, Cepeda led the N.L. with 46 home runs while leading the majors with 142 RBIs. He was the first player born outside the US to lead his league in home runs. Cepeda hit .300 or better in six of his first seven seasons before suffering a knee injury in 1965 that would linger throughout his career. It occurred at a time when he was competing for playing time at first base with future Hall of Famer and previous Rookie of the Year Willie McCovey.

The Cardinals May 1966 trade for Cepeda filled the gap they had at first base on a team that would win the 1967 and 1968 NL pennants. Cepeda embraced his new team and became a leading force on and off the field. In the clubhouse his pranks and music earned him the nickname "Cha-Cha." On the field Cepeda took charge in that first pennant-winning season, batting .325 with 25 homers and an N.L. best 111 RBIs as the Redbird cleanup hitter.

While the team was winning another pennant in 1968, Cepeda was having an off year at the plate. In a surprise move, the Cardinals traded him to Atlanta in 1969 for future Hall of Famer Joe Torre. Cepeda hit well in Atlanta, but continued trouble with his knee limited his time in the field. The A.L.'s 1973 adoption of the designated hitter led to one last honor as Cepeda became the first recipient of the Designated Hitter of the Year Award with the Red Sox.

Wikimedia Commons

Inducted into the Hall of Fame as a player in 1999 by the Veterans Committee

Position: *First Base*

Batted: *Right* **Threw:** *Right*

Height: *6' 2"* **Weight:** *210 lbs.*

Born: *September 17, 1937, in Ponce, Puerto Rico*

Died: *June 28, 2024, in Concord, CA*

Buried: *Cementerio Municipal Viejo, Juncos, Puerto Rico*

Debut: *April 15, 1958, with the San Francisco Giants*

Final game: *September 19, 1974, with the Kansas City Royals*

Postseason: *World Series Champion (1967), 3× N.L. Pennant (1962, 1967, 1968)*

Awards & Recognition: *11x All-Star (1959 twice, 1960 twice, 1961 twice, 1962 twice, 1963, 1964, 1967), N.L. Rookie of the Year (1958), N.L. Home Run Leader (1961), 2× N.L. RBI Leader (1961, 1967), N.L. MVP (1967)*

Nicknames: *Baby Bull, Cha Cha*

Numbers worn in St. Louis: *Cardinals (28, 30)*

Orlando Cepeda – HOF Playing Stats – WAR: 50.1, Slash Line: .297 / .350 / .499

SEASON	TEAM	LG	G	AB	R	H	2B	3B	HR	RBI	SB	BB	SO	BA
1958	SFG	NL	148	603	88	188	38	4	25	96	15	29	84	.312
1959	SFG	NL	151	605	92	192	35	4	27	105	23	33	100	.317
1960	SFG	NL	151	569	81	169	36	3	24	96	15	34	91	.297
1961	SFG	NL	152	585	105	182	28	4	46	142	12	39	91	.311
1962	SFG	NL	162	625	105	191	26	1	35	114	10	37	97	.306
1963	SFG	NL	156	579	100	183	33	4	34	97	8	37	70	.316
1964	SFG	NL	142	529	75	161	27	2	31	97	9	43	83	.304
1965	SFG	NL	33	34	1	6	1	0	1	5	0	3	9	.176
1966	SFG	NL	19	49	5	14	2	0	3	15	0	4	11	.286
1966	**STL**	**NL**	**123**	**452**	**65**	**137**	**24**	**0**	**17**	**58**	**9**	**34**	**68**	**.303**
1967	**STL**	**NL**	**151**	**563**	**91**	**183**	**37**	**0**	**25**	**111**	**11**	**62**	**75**	**.325**
1968	**STL**	**NL**	**157**	**600**	**71**	**149**	**26**	**2**	**16**	**73**	**8**	**43**	**96**	**.248**
1969	ATL	NL	154	573	74	147	28	2	22	88	12	55	76	.257
1970	ATL	NL	148	567	87	173	33	0	34	111	6	47	75	.305
1971	ATL	NL	71	250	31	69	10	1	14	44	3	22	29	.276
1972	ATL	NL	28	84	6	25	3	0	4	9	0	7	17	.298
1972	OAK	AL	3	3	0	0	0	0	0	0	0	0	0	.000
1973	BOS	AL	142	550	51	159	25	0	20	86	0	50	81	.289
1974	KCR	AL	33	107	3	23	5	0	1	18	1	9	16	.215
Career Totals			**2124**	**7927**	**1131**	**2351**	**417**	**27**	**379**	**1365**	**142**	**588**	**1169**	**.297**
STL (3 Yrs)		**NL**	**431**	**1615**	**227**	**469**	**87**	**2**	**58**	**242**	**28**	**139**	**239**	**.290**

State Historical Society of Missouri

Ozzie Smith

Ozzie Smith's nickname, "the Wizard of Oz," was the perfect play on his first name combined with his sorcery on the field. His Hall of Fame plaque says Smith "revolutionized defensive play at shortstop with his acrobatic fielding and artistic turning of double plays." He struck gold (as in gloves) 13 times as the NL's best shortstop. When he retired from the game, he held six fielding records at shortstop, including most assists, double plays, and chances accepted. Ozzie was quoted saying "I may not drive in 100 runs a year, but I can prevent 100 runs from scoring against us." He became the cornerstone of the Redbirds' strong defense and winning ways of the 1980s.

Defense got Ozzie to the big leagues with the San Diego Padres in 1978. But by the end of his career, the Wizard had become more than just a gold glove. With the Cardinals playing in three World Series in six years, Smith became a legend. To start each season's opening game and every postseason game Ozzie responded to the fans' chant of "Ozzzie–Ozzzie." with his celebrated backflip. And then there was the day when Hall of Fame Cardinal broadcaster Jack Buck shouted the iconic phrase, "Go crazy folks, go crazy!" after Ozzie homered for a walk-off win during a key playoff game in 1985 against the Dodgers. Magically, that blast was the first home run in the switch-hitting Smith's career from the left side of the plate (a span of 3,009 at bats). During that same 1985 season Smith had raised his batting average to a career high of .276; he would raise it to .303 in 1987, when he finished as runner-up in the N.L. MVP race. He was no longer just a light-hitting shortstop. This 15-time All-Star collected 2,460 hits during his 19-season career while batting .262 to go along with 580 stolen bases.

Wikimedia Commons

Inducted into the Hall of Fame as a player in 2002 (first ballot) by the BBWAA

Position: *Shortstop*

Batted: *Both* **Threw:** *Right*

Height: *5' 11"* **Weight:** *150 lbs.*

Born: *December 26, 1954, in Mobile, AL*

Debut: *April 7, 1978, with the San Diego Padres*

Final game: *September 29, 1996, with the St. Louis Cardinals*

Postseason: *World Series Champion (1982), 3× N.L. Pennant (1982, 1985, 1987)*

Awards & Recognition: *15× All-Star (1981–1992, 1994–1996), 13× Gold Glove Award (1980–1992), NLCS MVP (1987), Silver Slugger Award, (1987), Roberto Clemente Award (1995)*

Nickname: *The Wizard of Oz*

Number worn in St. Louis: *Cardinals (1–Retired)*

Ozzie Smith – HOF Playing Stats – WAR: 76.9, Slash Line: .262 / .337 / .328

SEASON	TEAM	LG	G	AB	R	H	2B	3B	HR	RBI	SB	BB	SO	BA
1978	SDP	NL	159	590	69	152	17	6	1	46	40	47	43	.258
1979	SDP	NL	156	587	77	124	18	6	0	27	28	37	37	.211
1980	SDP	NL	158	609	67	140	18	5	0	35	57	71	49	.230
1981	SDP	NL	110	450	53	100	11	2	0	21	22	41	37	.222
1982	STL	NL	140	488	58	121	24	1	2	43	25	68	32	.248
1983	STL	NL	159	552	69	134	30	6	3	50	34	64	36	.243
1984	STL	NL	124	412	53	106	20	5	1	44	35	56	17	.257
1985	STL	NL	158	537	70	148	22	3	6	54	31	65	27	.276
1986	STL	NL	153	514	67	144	19	4	0	54	31	79	27	.280
1987	STL	NL	158	600	104	182	40	4	0	75	43	89	36	.303
1988	STL	NL	153	575	80	155	27	1	3	51	57	74	43	.270
1989	STL	NL	155	593	82	162	30	8	2	50	29	55	37	.273
1990	STL	NL	143	512	61	130	21	1	1	50	32	61	33	.254
1991	STL	NL	150	550	96	157	30	3	3	50	35	83	36	.285
1992	STL	NL	132	518	73	153	20	2	0	31	43	59	34	.295
1993	STL	NL	141	545	75	157	22	6	1	53	21	43	18	.288
1994	STL	NL	98	381	51	100	18	3	3	30	6	38	26	.262
1995	STL	NL	44	156	16	31	5	1	0	11	4	17	12	.199
1996	STL	NL	82	227	36	64	10	2	2	18	7	25	9	.282
Career Totals			2573	9396	1257	2460	402	69	28	793	580	1072	589	.262
STL (15 Yrs)		NL	1990	7160	991	1944	338	50	27	664	433	876	423	.272

Getty Images

Dennis Eckersley

Known simply as "Eck" to most baseball fans, Dennis Eckersley made one of baseball's most amazing pitching transformations. He evolved from one of the game'sbest starting pitchers to one of the best relievers in all of baseball. He became the only pitcher in MLB history with 100 saves (actually 390) and 100 complete games while posting a 197–171 record. Ten times he recorded double-digit win totals, including a 20-win season in 1978. He even threw a no-hitter in 1977.

His transformation began in 1987 following his trade by the Cubs to the Athletics. Under the tutelage of manager Tony La Russa and pitching coach Dave Duncan, "Eck" moved from the starting rotation to the bullpen. In the last 12 seasons of his 24-year career, he would only start two of his final 695 games.

Eckersley's Hall of Fame plaque credits his success to a "combined blazing fastball and devastating slider, pinpoint control and a deceptive sidearm delivery." It was a combination that saved 320 games for his new Oakland team. Between 1988 and 1992 the Athletics became one of baseball's premier teams, winning four division titles on their way to three pennants and the 1989 World Championship. In 1990 Eckersley only allowed five earned runs in 73.1 innings pitched. In 1992, his pitching feats earned him the A.L.'s Cy Young and MVP Awards.

In 1996, Eck's mentors La Russa and Duncan joined the Cardinals and immediately made a trade to bring their bullpen ace to St. Louis. Even though he posted a 0–6 record that year, Eckersley contributed 30 saves as the Redbirds won their first Division title since 1987. The Cardinals were not a winning team the next year, and Eck went 1–5 with 36 saves before leaving the team as a free agent to return once more to Boston to finish his career.

Getty Images

Inducted into the Hall of Fame as a player in 2004 (first ballot) by the BBWAA

Position: *Pitcher*

Batted: *Right* **Threw:** *Right*

Height: *6' 2"* **Weight:** *190 lbs.*

Born: *October 3, 1954, in Oakland, CA*

Debut: *April 12, 1975, with the Cleveland Indians*

Final game: *September 26, 1998, with the Boston Red Sox*

Postseason: *World Series Champion (1989), 3× A.L. Pennant (1988, 1989, 1990)*

Awards & Recognition: *6× All-Star (1977, 1982, 1988, 1990–1992), A.L. MVP (1992), A.L. Cy Young Award (1992), ALCS MVP (1992), 2× A.L. Rolaids Relief Man Award (1988, 1992)*

Nickname: *Eck*

Number worn in St. Louis: *Cardinals (43)*

Dennis Eckersley – HOF Career Playing Stats – WAR: 62.1

YEAR(S)	SEASONS	TEAM	LEAGUE	W	L	ERA	G	CG	SHO	SV	IP	H	HR	BB	SO
1984 - 1986	3	CLE	AL	40	32	3.23	103	27	8	3	633.1	516	60	222	543
1978 - 1984, 1998	8	BOS	AL	88	71	3.92	241	64	10	1	1371.2	1408	167	312	771
1984 - 1986	3	CHC	AL	27	26	3.63	82	9	2	0	530.2	523	47	98	335
1987 - 1995	9	OAK	AL	41	31	2.74	525	0	0	320	637	515	56	92	658
1996 - 1997	**2**	**STL**	**NL**	**1**	**11**	**3.58**	**120**	**0**	**0**	**66**	**113**	**114**	**17**	**14**	**94**
Career Totals	24			197	171	3.50	1071	100	20	390	3285.2	3076	347	738	2401

Getty Images

Bruce Sutter

As the baseball saying goes, "good pitching beats good hitting." In the early 1980s Bruce Sutter offered a corollary: "Great relief pitching wins ballgames, and even a World Series." Sutter would become the first pitcher to reach the Hall of Fame without ever starting a major league game. From his first game with the Cubs in 1976 through his next 660 games, there was never a single start; he instead recorded 300 saves. His dominance earned him not only the NL's 1979 Cy Young Award, but also four N.L. Fireman of the Year awards (1979, 1981, 1982, and 1984).

Sutter's career underwent a Cinderella transformation after a 1972 arm injury cast doubt on his making the major leagues. Still in the minors following surgery, Sutter punched his ticket to the major leagues under the tutelage of the Cubs' minor league pitching coach Fred Martin. Over the next three seasons he mastered a new pitch: the split-fingered fastball. The pitch became effective when Sutter's thumb pushed the ball out from between wide-spread fingers to impart a sharp forward spin on the ball. With the look of a normal fastball, it suddenly dove down through the strike zone as the pitch neared the plate.

Sutter brought the pitch to the majors in 1976, and by 1977 he made the first of five straight All-Star game appearances. He would win or save four consecutive All-Star games (1978 to 1981) and receive another selection to the Midseason Classic in 1984. In 1979 Sutter won the Cy Young Award and tied the N.L. record with 37 saves, leading the majors. He would be the N.L. saves leader for the next three seasons while once more leading the majors in 1982 with 36 saves as a Cardinal. But for most St. Louis fans Sutter's best moment came in the ninth inning of the seventh game of the 1982 World Series with two out and two strikes. The Milwaukee Brewers' Gorman Thomas stood at the plate waiting for Sutter's delivery. Legendary broadcaster Jack Buck summed it up well, "Sutter from the belt, to the plate . . . a swing and a miss! And that's a winner! That's a winner! A World Series winner for the Cardinals!"

Getty Images

Inducted into the Hall of Fame as a player in 2006 by the BBWAA

Position: *Pitcher*

Batted: *Right* **Threw:** *Right*

Height: *6' 2"* **Weight:** *190 lbs.*

Born: *January 8, 1953, in Lancaster, PA*

Died: *October 13, 2022, in Cartersville, GA*

Buried: *Unknown*

Debut: *May 9, 1975, with the Chicago Cubs*

Final game: *September 9, 1988, with the Atlanta Braves*

Postseason: *World Series Champion (1982), N.L. Pennant (1982)*

Awards & Recognition: *6× All-Star (1977–1981, 1984), N.L. Cy Young Award (1979), 4× Rolaids Relief Man Award (1979, 1981, 1982, 1984), 5× N.L. Saves Leader (1979–1982, 1984)*

Number worn in St. Louis: *Cardinals (42–Retired)*

Bruce Sutter – HOF Pitching Stats – WAR: 24.0

YEAR	TEAM	LG	W	L	ERA	G	CG	SHO	SV	IP	H	HR	BB	SO
1976	CHC	NL	6	3	2.70	52	0	0	10	83.1	63	4	26	73
1977	CHC	NL	7	3	1.34	62	0	0	31	107.1	69	5	23	129
1978	CHC	NL	8	10	3.19	64	0	0	27	98.2	82	10	34	106
1979	CHC	NL	6	6	2.22	62	0	0	37	101.1	67	3	32	110
1980	CHC	NL	5	8	2.64	60	0	0	28	102.1	90	5	34	76
1981	**STL**	**NL**	**3**	**5**	**2.62**	**48**	**0**	**0**	**25**	**82.1**	**64**	**5**	**24**	**57**
1982	**STL**	**NL**	**9**	**8**	**2.90**	**70**	**0**	**0**	**36**	**102.1**	**88**	**8**	**34**	**61**
1983	**STL**	**NL**	**9**	**10**	**4.23**	**60**	**0**	**0**	**21**	**89.1**	**90**	**8**	**30**	**64**
1984	**STL**	**NL**	**5**	**7**	**1.54**	**71**	**0**	**0**	**45**	**122.2**	**109**	**9**	**23**	**77**
1985	ATL	NL	7	7	4.48	58	0	0	23	88.1	91	13	29	52
1986	ATL	NL	2	0	4.34	16	0	0	3	18.2	17	3	9	16
1988	ATL	NL	1	4	4.76	38	0	0	14	45.1	49	4	11	40
Career Totals			**68**	**71**	**2.83**	**661**	**0**	**0**	**300**	**1042**	**879**	**77**	**309**	**861**
STL (4 yrs)		**NL**	**26**	**30**	**2.72**	**249**	**0**	**0**	**127**	**396.2**	**351**	**30**	**111**	**259**

Getty Images

Billy Southworth

Teams often emulate their managers. Billy Southworth was a winner, and so were his teams. He never had a losing season in the nine full seasons he managed. Six times his teams won more than 90 games while winning four pennants and two World Series titles. He is one of only two Cardinal skippers to win two championships.

Southworth spent 13 seasons in the majors playing for five different teams before becoming a manager. Three of those seasons were with the Cardinals, including their 1926 Championship season. Southworth also played in the 1924 World Series with the New York Giants. After injuries limited Southworth's play in 1927, Branch Rickey offered him a position as a player–manager in the farm system. In 1929 Rickey's managerial revolving door sent the previous year's pennant-winning skipper (Bill McKechnie) out and brought Southworth up from the minors. Managing his former teammates became a challenge, and after 89 games the door swung McKechnie back in as manager and sent Southworth back to the minors until he was called to lead the Cardinals during the 1940 season.

With the help of quality players from Rickey's farm system, Southworth's teams would soon win at least 105 games and three straight pennants (1942, 1943, 1944) in a three-year stretch that included two World Series Championships. No other team in baseball history has ever had such a winning streak. His .642 winning percentage leads all Cardinal managers since 1900. After finishing three games back in second place in 1945 (due in part to Stan Musial's time serving in the navy), Southworth was coxed to manage and rebuild the Boston Braves with a three-year contract that the Cardinals could not afford to match. His efforts paid off when Boston won the N.L. pennant in 1948. When Southworth retired three years later, his managerial winning percentage of .597 was fifth best in the history of the game. Today it ranks 12th.

Wikimedia Commons

Inducted into the Hall of Fame as a manager in 2008 by the Veterans Committee

Positions: *Right Field, Manager*

Batted: *Left* **Threw:** *Right*

Height: *5' 9"* **Weight:** *170 lbs.*

Born: *March 9, 1893, in Harvard, NE*

Died: *November 15, 1969, in Columbus, OH*

Buried: *Green Lawn Cemetery, Columbus, OH*

Debut: *August 4, 1913, with the Cleveland Indians*

Final game: *July 9, 1929, with the St. Louis Cardinals*

Postseason: *3× World Series Champion (Player—1926, Manager—1942, 1944), 6× N.L. Pennant (Player—1924, 1926, Manager—1942–1944, 1948)*

Awards & Recognition: *3× N.L. All-Star Team Manager (1943, 1944, 1949)*

Number worn in St. Louis: *Cardinals (30)*

Billy Southworth – HOF Career Managerial Stats

YEAR(S)	SEASONS	TEAM	LEAGUE	WON	LOST	W-L%	TIES	GAMES	EJECTIONS	PENNANTS	CHAMPIONSHIPS
1929, 1940 - 1945	**7**	**STL**	**Nl**	**620**	**346**	**.642**	**15**	**981**	**3**	**3**	**2**
1946 - 1951	6	BSN	NL	424	358	.542	7	789	2	1	0
Career Totals	13			1044	704	.597	22	1770	5	4	2

Billy Southworth – Career Playing Stats – WAR: 21.7, Slash Line: .297 / .359 / .415

YEAR(S)	SEASONS	TEAM	LEAGUE	G	AB	R	H	2B	3B	HR	RBI	SB	BB	SO	BA
1913, 1915	2	CLE	AL	61	177	25	39	2	5	0	8	2	36	12	.220
1918 - 1920	3	PIT	NL	331	1245	157	366	36	34	8	157	65	110	51	.294
1921 - 1923	3	BSN	NL	337	1338	208	421	58	35	17	175	40	115	37	.315
1924 - 1926	3	NYG	NL	253	870	142	248	38	6	14	110	8	90	28	.285
1926 - 1927, 1929	**3**	**STL**	**NL**	**210**	**729**	**129**	**222**	**39**	**11**	**13**	**111**	**23**	**51**	**20**	**.305**
Career Totals	13			1192	4359	661	1296	173	91	52	561	138	402	148	.297

Cardinals manager Billy Southworth meets Browns owner Donald Barnes at the 1944 World Series.
St. Louis Browns Historical Society

Whitey Herzog

Dorrell Herzog's nickname of "Whitey" led to the style of baseball his teams played becoming known as "Whiteyball." It was an approach that won six division titles, three pennants, and one World Series during managerial stints in Kansas City and St. Louis. Whitey's career in baseball touched all the bases as a player, coach, scout, general manager, and farm system director. However, it was his managerial accomplishments that put him in the Hall of Fame.

Whitey spent eight seasons as a journeyman outfielder for four different teams before becoming the Mets director of player development. His oversight helped the team to two pennants (1969, 1973). When Yogi Berra was selected to manage the Mets after the sudden death of Gil Hodges, a snubbed Herzog was chosen to replace Ted Williams as manager of the Texas Rangers. Fired before his first season ended, Herzog coached the California Angels and became their interim manager before guiding the Kansas City Royals to three straight division titles from 1976 to 1978.

In the middle of the 1980 season Herzog was brought to St. Louis to turn around a last-place team. Holding both the on-field manager and general manager titles, Whitey rebuilt the Cardinals to take advantage of the spacious dimensions and artificial turf of Busch Stadium. He fielded a team focused on pitching, speed, and defense. With Whiteyball in place in 1981 the Redbirds didn't make the playoffs despite having the best record in their division. That year's midseason player's strike resulted in a unique playoff schedule based upon standings in the two halves of the season rather than the total season.

Herzog's Cardinals got their revenge the following year as they won the team's first pennant and World Series in 18 years. Whitey's Redbirds would win two more pennants in 1985 and 1987 and go the distance before losing each Series in the seventh game. Whitey's 822 wins and 728 loses each rank as the third highest totals in Cardinals' history. "Whitey Ball" brought some of the most exciting and winningest seasons in Cardinal history.

Inducted into the Hall of Fame as a manager in 2010 by the Veterans Committee

Positions: *Outfielder, First Base, Manager*

Batted: *Left* **Threw:** *Left*

Height: *5' 11"* **Weight:** *182 lbs.*

Born: *November 9, 1931, in New Athens, IL*

Died: *April 15, 2024, in St. Louis, MO*

Buried: *Cremated*

Debut: *April 17, 1956, with the Washington Senators*

Final game: *September 28, 1963, with the Detroit Tigers*

Postseason: *World Series Champion (1982), 3× N.L. Pennant (1982, 1985, 1987)*

Awards & Recognition: *M.L. Manager of the Year (1985), 3× N.L. All-Star Team Manager (1983, 1986, 1988)*

Nickname: *The White Rat*

Numbers worn in St. Louis: *Cardinals (3, 24—Retired)*

Whitey Herzog – HOF Career Managerial Stats

YEAR(S)	SEASONS	TEAM	LEAGUE	WON	LOST	W-L%	TIES	GAMES	EJECTIONS	PENNANTS	CHAMPIONSHIPS
1973	1	TEX	AL	47	91	.341	0	138	6	0	0
1974	1	CAL	AL	2	2	.500	0	4	0	0	0
1975 - 1979	5	KCR	AL	410	304	.574	0	714	13	0	0
1980-1990	**11**	**STL**	**NL**	**822**	**728**	**.530**	**3**	**1553**	**23**	**3**	**1**
Career Totals	**18**			**1281**	**1125**	**.532**	**3**	**2409**	**42**	**3**	**1**

Whitey Herzog – Career Playing Stats – WAR: 2.8, Slash Line: .257 / .354 / .365

YEAR(S)	SEASONS	TEAM	LEAGUE	G	AB	R	H	2B	3B	HR	RBI	SB	BB	SO	BA
1956 - 1958	3	WSH	AL	161	504	56	116	16	7	4	39	9	49	91	.230
1958 - 1960	3	KCA	AL	209	471	79	126	18	5	9	56	1	90	76	.268
1961 - 1962	2	BAL	AL	212	586	73	164	24	7	12	70	3	91	77	.280
1963	1	DET	AL	52	53	5	8	2	1	0	7	0	11	17	.151
Career Totals	**8**			**634**	**1614**	**213**	**414**	**60**	**20**	**25**	**172**	**13**	**241**	**261**	**.257**

Getty Images

Tony La Russa

Tony La Russa's baseball career began as a journeyman infielder (hitting .199 for three teams) and ended as baseball's second-winningest manager. During his 35 years as a manager he guided three teams to World Series titles and won six pennants and 13 division titles. His total of 2,884 wins over 35 years is second only to Connie Mack's 3,731 wins across 53 seasons. Mack also tops the leaderboard in losses (3,948), with La Russa second (2,499). Both are the only managers to win World Championships across three decades.

La Russa's managerial career began at age 34 with the White Sox in 1979. Four years later his club won their Division and La Russa was named the A.L. Manager of the Year. Fired midseason in 1986, La Russa joined the Oakland Athletics and within a year turned them into a winning team. They made their first of three consecutive appearances in the World Series in 1988 (winning in 1989). La Russa again won the A.L. Manager of the Year that year and would win it a third time after his team won another division title in 1992.

In 1996, La Russa became manager of the Cardinals and immediately put them in the playoffs after an eight-year absence before losing the N.L. Championship Series in seven games. He would go on to become the franchise's winningest skipper with 1,408 victories. La Russa's Redbirds would win six Central Division titles between 2000 and 2009 and three N.L. pennants in 2004, 2006, and 2011—the latter two being World Championships. He would pick up a fourth Manager of the Year Award in 2002.

La Russa enhanced baseball through his managerial strategies. His Hall of Fame plaque recognizes him as "a master of maneuvering lineups and managing bullpens," most notably the development of the one-inning closer. His machinations made him "the first manager ever to win an All-Star game in each league and the second to win the World Series in each.

Inducted into the Hall of Fame as a manager in 2014 by the Expansion Era Committee

Positions: *Infield, Manager*

Batted: *Right* **Threw:** *Right*

Height: *6' 0"* **Weight:** *175 lbs.*

Born: *October 4, 1944, in Tampa, FL*

Debut: *May 10, 1963, with the Kansas City Athletics*

Final game: *April 6, 1973, with the Chicago Cubs*

Postseason: *3× World Series Champion (1989, 2006, 2011), 3× A.L. Pennant (1988, 1989, 1990), 3x N.L. Pennant (2004, 2006, 2011)*

Awards & Recognition: *4× Manager of the Year (1983, 1988, 1992, 2002)*

Number worn in St. Louis: *Cardinals (10—Retired)*

Tony La Russa – HOF Career Managerial Stats

YEAR(S)	SEASONS	TEAM	LEAGUE	WON	LOST	W-L%	TIES	GAMES	EJECTIONS	PENNANTS	CHAMPIONSHIPS
1979 - 1986, 2021 - 2022	11	CHW	AL	678	644	.513	3	1325	32	0	0
1986 - 1995	10	OAK	AL	798	673	.542	0	1471	22	3	1
1996 - 2011	**16**	**STL**	**NL**	**1408**	**1182**	**.544**	**1**	**2591**	**39**	**3**	**2**
Career Totals	**35**			**2884**	**2499**	**.536**	**4**	**5387**	**93**	**6**	**3**

Tony La Russa – Career Playing Stats – WAR: -0.6, Slash Line: .199 / .292 / .250

YEAR(S)	SEASONS	TEAM	LEAGUE	G	AB	R	H	2B	3B	HR	RBI	SB	BB	SO	BA
1963, 1968 - 1971	5	KCA / OAK	AL	122	169	13	33	5	2	0	7	0	22	36	.195
1971	1	ATL	NL	9	7	1	2	0	0	0	0	0	1	1	.286
1973	1	CHC	NL	1	0	1	0	0	0	0	0	0	0	0	.000
Career Totals	**6**			**132**	**176**	**15**	**35**	**5**	**2**	**0**	**7**	**0**	**23**	**37**	**.199**

Wikimedia Commons

Joe Torre

Joe Torre excelled in the field, in the dugout, and later in Major League Baseball's front office. He was an All-Star nine times in 18 seasons playing the game. While the Braves remember Torre as Milwaukee's runner-up Rookie-of-the-Year behind the plate in 1961, St. Louisans remember that magical season a decade later when Torre hit .363 to win the 1971 N.L. MVP at third base. He also led the league in hits and RBIs that year. His six seasons with the Cardinals, in which he batted .308, were the best of his career. Despite his success on the field, Torre never played in a World Series.

He switched from the field to the dugout in 1977 during his final year playing for the Mets. After five years in which the team failed to win more than 70 games in a season, the Mets fired Torre. Hired to manage the Braves in 1982, Torre led them to that year's N.L. Championship game. His shot at a World Series was denied by his former team, the Cardinals.

Fired by the Braves in 1984, Torre became a television commentator with the Angels. Following Whitey Herzog's sudden resignation in 1990, Torre was brought back to St. Louis to manage the Cardinals. He had now managed the three teams on which he played. Despite several winning seasons with the Redbirds, Torre could not guide them to the playoffs and was dismissed in the 1995 season prior to the team being sold.

In 1996 Torre made it to the World Series as manager of George Steinbrenner's Yankees. He would make six trips to the Fall Classic and win four Championships and two Manager of the Year awards. How successful was Torre's time managing in the city of his birth? He took the Yankees to the postseason in each of his 12 seasons with the team.

Getty Images

Inducted into the Hall of Fame as a manager in 2014 by the Expansion Era Committee

Positions: *Catcher, First Base, Third Base, Manager*

Batted: *Right* **Threw:** *Right*

Height: *6' 2"* **Weight:** *212 lbs.*

Born: *July 18, 1940, in Brooklyn, NY*

Debut: *September 25, 1960, with the Milwaukee Braves*

Final game: *June 17, 1977, with the New York Mets*

Postseason: *4x World Series Champion (1996, 1998–2000), 5× A.L. Pennant (1996, 1998–2001, 2003)*

Awards & Recognition: *9× All-Star (1953–1967, 1970–1973), Gold Glove Award (1965), N.L. MVP (1971), N.L. RBI Leader (1971), 2× A.L. Manager of the Year (1996, 1998)*

Number worn in St. Louis: *Cardinals (9)*

Joe Torre – HOF Career Managerial Stats

YEAR(S)	SEASONS	TEAM	LEAGUE	WON	LOST	W-L%	TIES	GAMES	EJECTIONS	PENNANTS	CHAMPIONSHIPS
1977 - 1981	5	NYM	NL	286	420	.405	3	709	24	0	0
1982 -1984	3	ATL	NL	257	229	.529	0	486	5	0	0
1990 - 1995	**6**	**STL**	**NL**	**351**	**354**	**.498**	**1**	**706**	**15**	**0**	**0**
1996 - 2007	12	NYY	AL	1173	767	.605	2	1942	22	6	4
2008 - 2010	3	LAD	NL	259	227	.533	0	486	4	0	0
Career Totals	**29**			**2326**	**1997**	**.538**	**6**	**4329**	**70**	**6**	**4**

Joe Torre – Career Playing Stats – WAR: 57.6, Slash Line: .297 / .365 / .452

YEAR(S)	SEASONS	TEAM	LEAGUE	G	AB	R	H	2B	3B	HR	RBI	SB	BB	SO	BA
1960 - 1968	9	MLN / ATL	NL	1037	3700	470	1087	154	21	142	552	10	334	518	.294
1969 - 1974	**6**	**STL**	**NL**	**918**	**3452**	**455**	**1062**	**161**	**32**	**98**	**558**	**12**	**387**	**476**	**.308**
1975 - 1977	3	NYM	NL	254	722	71	193	29	6	12	75	1	58	100	.267
Career Totals	**18**			**2209**	**7874**	**996**	**2342**	**344**	**59**	**252**	**1185**	**23**	**779**	**1094**	**.297**

Missouri Historical Society, St. Louis

John Smoltz

How does John Smoltz fit in a book about Hall of Famers with ties to St. Louis? It's because he pitched seven games for the Cardinals during the 2009 season. It was in his 21st and final season, and he had just been released by the Boston Red Sox. Those seven games were the final outings of his 723-game major league career. He signed with St. Louis after his August release as the Central Division–leading Cardinals were strengthening their bullpen for the playoffs.

In his first game with the Redbirds against the Padres, Smoltz set a franchise record by striking out seven consecutive batters to get his first win with the team. He would win no more, and his record was 1–3 going into the playoffs. He pitched two innings of relief in a Game 3 loss to the Dodgers for his final MLB appearance. After leaving the mound, Smoltz became a leading baseball television commentator.

Before coming to St. Louis, Smoltz was one of the most dominating pitchers in the game during the 1990s and early 2000s. Like Dennis Eckersley, Smoltz transformed from an electric starting pitcher to one of the game's best out of the bullpen. While Smoltz is the only pitcher to win at least 200 games and record 150 saves, it does not compare to Eckersley's 197 wins and 390 saves. They were both special and won in different ways.

Smoltz was part of the Atlanta Braves' dynasty led by a duo of Cy Young Award (CYA) pitchers Greg Maddox (four CYAs) and Tom Glavine (two CYAs). They formed a trio with Smoltz (one CYA) to lead the team to 14 consecutive division championships from 1991 to 2005. It makes one wonder how many CYAs Smoltz could have won that were instead given to his teammates.

Wikimedia Commons

Inducted into the Hall of Fame as a player in 2015 (first ballot) by the BBWAA

Position: *Pitcher*

Batted: *Right* **Threw:** *Right*

Height: *6' 3"* **Weight:** *210 lbs.*

Born: *May 15, 1967, in Warren, MI*

Debut: *July 23, 1988, with the Atlanta Braves*

Final game: *September 30, 2009, with the St. Louis Cardinals*

Postseason: *World Series Champion (1995), 5× N.L. Pennant (1991, 1992, 1995, 1996, 1999)*

Awards & Recognition: *8× All-Star (1989, 1992, 1993, 1996, 2002, 2003, 2005, 2007), NLCS MVP (1992), N.L. Cy Young Award (1996), Silver Slugger Award (1997), N.L. Rolaids Relief Man Award (2002), 2× N.L. Wins Leader (1992, 1996), N.L. Saves Leader (2002)*

Nickname: *Smoltzie*

Number worn in St. Louis: *Cardinals (30)*

John Smoltz – HOF Pitching Stats – WAR: 69.0

YEAR	TM	LG	W	L	ERA	G	CG	SHO	SV	IP	ER	HR	BB	SO
1988	ATL	NL	2	7	5.48	12	0	0	0	64	39	10	33	37
1989	ATL	NL	12	11	2.94	29	5	0	0	208	68	15	72	168
1990	ATL	NL	14	11	3.85	34	6	2	0	231.1	99	20	90	170
1991	ATL	NL	14	13	3.80	36	5	0	0	229.2	97	16	77	148
1992	ATL	NL	15	12	2.85	35	9	3	0	246.2	78	17	80	215
1993	ATL	NL	15	11	3.62	35	3	1	0	243.2	98	23	100	208
1994	ATL	NL	6	10	4.14	21	1	0	0	134.2	62	15	48	113
1995	ATL	NL	12	7	3.18	29	2	1	0	192.2	68	15	72	193
1996	ATL	NL	24	8	2.94	35	6	2	0	253.2	83	19	55	276
1997	ATL	NL	15	12	3.02	35	7	2	0	256	86	21	63	241
1998	ATL	NL	17	3	2.90	26	2	2	0	167.2	54	10	44	173
1999	ATL	NL	11	8	3.19	29	1	1	0	186.1	66	14	40	156
2000	Did not play in major or minor leagues (injured)													
2001	ATL	NL	3	3	3.36	36	0	0	10	59	22	7	10	57
2002	ATL	NL	3	2	3.25	75	0	0	55	80.1	29	4	24	85
2003	ATL	NL	0	2	1.12	62	0	0	45	64.1	8	2	8	73
2004	ATL	NL	0	1	2.76	73	0	0	44	81.2	25	8	13	85
2005	ATL	NL	14	7	3.06	33	3	1	0	229.2	78	18	53	169
2006	ATL	NL	16	9	3.49	35	3	1	0	232	90	23	55	211
2007	ATL	NL	14	8	3.11	32	0	0	0	205.2	71	18	47	197
2008	ATL	NL	3	2	2.57	6	0	0	0	28	8	2	8	36
2009	BOS	AL	2	5	8.33	8	0	0	0	40	37	8	9	33
2009	**STL**	**NL**	**1**	**3**	**4.26**	**7**	**0**	**0**	**0**	**38**	**18**	**3**	**9**	**40**
Career Totals			**213**	**ol**	**3.33**	**723**	**53**	**16**	**154**	**3473**	**1284**	**288**	**1010**	**3084**
STL (1 yr)		**NL**	**1**	**3**	**4.26**	**7**	**0**	**0**	**0**	**38**	**18**	**3**	**9**	**40**

Wikimedia Commons

Lee Smith

Lee Smith retired from baseball on top. The six-foot five-inch righthander with the blazing fastball left the game in 1997 with the most saves ever recorded. He saved 478 games over an 18-year career playing for eight different teams. Ironically, Smith nearly quit the game because he didn't want to be a reliever. He wanted to be a starter. Relieving turned out quite well for the big man with the nasty scowl that hitters feared. He became the first reliever in the game to reach 400 saves and would be the career saves leader for over a decade until topped on the leaderboard by Trever Hoffman (601 Saves) and Mariano Rivera (652 Saves).

The sight of the pitching giant on the mound throwing "pure gas" from the afternoon shadows (before Wrigley Field had lights) was enough to overwhelm any hitter. In his fourth season he led the N.L. in saves (29) for the first time and made his first All-Star appearance. A year later, in 1984, Smith helped the Cubs end their playoff drought. It would be the first of Smith's two postseason appearances, but neither produced a pennant or World Series. After reeling off more than 30 saves the next three seasons Smith became only the second reliever to ever reach that mark in four straight years.

After a stop in Boston following a 1987 trade, Smith was traded to St. Louis for Tom Brunansky in 1990. There he made three straight All-Star appearances and led baseball with 47 saves in 1991 and 43 the next year to became the N.L. career saves leader, passing Bruce Sutter's 300 saves. Traded to the Yankees during 1993's late-season playoff push, Smith left St. Louis as the franchise's all-time saves leader (160) until Jason Isringhausen recorded his 217 saves between 2002 and 2008.

Getty Images

Inducted into the Hall of Fame as a player in 2019 by the Today's Game Era Committee

Position: *Pitcher*

Batted: *Right* **Threw:** *Right*

Height: *6' 5"* **Weight:** *220 lbs.*

Born: *December 4, 1957, in Jamestown, LA*

Debut: *September 1, 1980, with the Chicago Cubs*

Final game: *July 2, 1997, with the Montreal Expos*

Postseason: *N/A*

Awards & Recognition: *7× All-Star (1983, 1987, 1991–1995), 3× Rolaids Relief Man Award (1991, 1992, 1994), 3× N.L Saves Leader (1983, 1991, 1992). A.L. Saves Leader (1994)*

Number worn in St. Louis: *Cardinals (47)*

Lee Smith – HOF Pitching Stats – WAR: 28.9

YEAR	TEAM	LG	W	L	ERA	G	CG	SHO	SV	IP	ER	HR	BB	SO
1980	CHC	NL	2	0	2.91	18	0	0	0	21.2	21	0	14	17
1981	CHC	NL	3	6	3.51	40	0	0	1	66.2	57	2	31	50
1982	CHC	NL	2	5	2.69	72	0	0	17	117	105	5	37	99
1983	CHC	NL	4	10	1.65	66	0	0	29	103.1	70	5	41	91
1984	CHC	NL	9	7	3.65	69	0	0	33	101	98	6	35	86
1985	CHC	NL	7	4	3.04	65	0	0	33	97.2	87	9	32	112
1986	CHC	NL	9	9	3.09	66	0	0	31	90.1	69	7	42	93
1987	CHC	NL	4	10	3.12	62	0	0	36	83.2	84	4	32	96
1988	BOS	AL	4	5	2.80	64	0	0	29	83.2	72	7	37	96
1989	BOS	AL	6	1	3.57	64	0	0	25	70.2	53	6	33	96
1990	BOS	AL	2	1	1.88	11	0	0	4	14.1	13	0	9	17
1990	**STL**	**NL**	**3**	**4**	**2.10**	**53**	**0**	**0**	**27**	**68.2**	**58**	**3**	**20**	**70**
1991	**STL**	**NL**	**6**	**3**	**2.34**	**67**	**0**	**0**	**47**	**73**	**70**	**5**	**13**	**67**
1992	**STL**	**NL**	**4**	**9**	**3.12**	**70**	**0**	**0**	**43**	**75**	**62**	**4**	**26**	**60**
1993	**STL**	**NL**	**2**	**4**	**4.50**	**55**	**0**	**0**	**43**	**50**	**49**	**11**	**9**	**49**
1993	NYY	AL	0	0	0.00	8	0	0	3	8	4	0	5	11
1994	BAL	AL	1	4	3.29	41	0	0	33	38.1	34	6	11	42
1995	CAL	AL	0	5	3.47	52	0	0	37	49.1	42	3	25	43
1996	TOT	MLB	3	4	3.74	54	0	0	2	55.1	57	4	26	41
1996	CAL	AL	0	0	2.45	11	0	0	0	11	8	0	3	6
1996	CIN	NL	3	4	4.06	43	0	0	2	44.1	49	4	23	35
1997	MON	NL	0	1	5.82	25	0	0	5	21.2	28	2	8	15
Career Totals			**71**	**92**	**3.03**	**1022**	**0**	**0**	**478**	**1289.1**	**1133**	**89**	**486**	**1251**
STL (4 Yrs)		**NL**	**15**	**20**	**2.90**	**245**	**0**	**0**	**160**	**266.2**	**239**	**23**	**68**	**246**

Getty Images

Ted Simmons

Any list of baseball's top five catchers of the 1970s will include Ted Simmons. During that decade he was one of the finest offensive catchers in the game—perhaps even one of the best of all time. When Simmons retired, he led all catchers in career hits and doubles. His 193 hits in 1975 were the most of any catcher who caught at least 150 games in a season. His 192 hits in 1973 ranked second on that same list. When he retired in 1988, he was second only to catchers Yogi Berra in career RBIs and Carlton Fisk in career total bases and was the N.L. home run leader (182) for switch-hitters—that's all switch-hitters, not just catchers. Simmons, along with the Negro Leagues' Biz Mackey, are the only switch-hitting catchers in the Hall of Fame.

With these stats, it is reasonable to question why it took Simmons so long to get the call to Cooperstown. He had his first taste of big-league baseball in a few games in 1968 at age 18. His first full season behind the plate was 1971. In that year and the six that followed, Simmons hit at least .303 five times and played in four All-Star games. He would get the nod to four more Midsummer Classics over the course of his 21-year career. While accomplishing much as a Cardinal, Simmons never made it to the playoffs or World Series.

But that changed after Simmons became a Milwaukee Brewer after the 1980 season. He was traded in one of manager Whitey Herzog's first moves to realign the Cardinals. The trade helped the Brewers make their first playoff appearance in 1981, and a year later they made their first World Series appearance. Unfortunately, it was against Simmons's former Cardinal team, which beat the Brewers in seven games.

Wikimedia Commons

Inducted into the Hall of Fame as a player in 2020 by the Modern Baseball Era Committee

Positions: *Catcher, First Base*

Batted: *Both* **Threw:** *Right*

Height: *5' 11"* **Weight:** *193 lbs.*

Born: *August 9, 1949, in Highland Park, MI*

Debut: *September 21, 1968, with the St. Louis Cardinals*

Final game: *October 2, 1988, with the Atlanta Braves*

Postseason: *A.L. Pennant (1982)*

Awards & Recognition: *8× All-Star (1972–1974, 1977–1979, 1981, 1983), Silver Slugger Award (1980)*

Nickname: *Simba*

Number worn in St. Louis: *Cardinals (23—Retired)*

Ted Simmons – HOF Playing Stats – WAR: 50.4, Slash Line: .285 / .348 / .437

SEASON	TEAM	LG	G	AB	R	H	2B	3B	HR	RBI	SB	BB	SO	BA
1968	STL	NL	2	3	0	1	0	0	0	0	0	1	1	.333
1969	STL	NL	5	14	0	3	0	1	0	3	0	1	1	.214
1970	STL	NL	82	284	29	69	8	2	3	24	2	37	37	.243
1971	STL	NL	133	510	64	155	32	4	7	77	1	36	50	.304
1972	STL	NL	152	594	70	180	36	6	16	96	1	29	57	.303
1973	STL	NL	161	619	62	192	36	2	13	91	2	61	47	.310
1974	STL	NL	152	599	66	163	33	6	20	103	0	47	35	.272
1975	STL	NL	157	581	80	193	32	3	18	100	1	63	35	.332
1976	STL	NL	150	546	60	159	35	3	5	75	0	73	35	.291
1977	STL	NL	150	516	82	164	25	3	21	95	2	79	37	.318
1978	STL	NL	152	516	71	148	40	5	22	80	1	77	39	.287
1979	STL	NL	123	448	68	127	22	0	26	87	0	61	34	.283
1980	STL	NL	145	495	84	150	33	2	21	98	1	59	45	.303
1981	MIL	AL	100	380	45	82	13	3	14	61	0	23	32	.216
1982	MIL	AL	137	539	73	145	29	0	23	97	0	32	40	.269
1983	MIL	AL	153	600	76	185	39	3	13	108	4	41	51	.308
1984	MIL	AL	132	497	44	110	23	2	4	52	3	30	40	.221
1985	MIL	AL	143	528	60	144	28	2	12	76	1	57	32	.273
1986	ATL	NL	76	127	14	32	5	0	4	25	1	12	14	.252
1987	ATL	NL	73	177	20	49	8	0	4	30	1	21	23	.277
1988	ATL	NL	78	107	6	21	6	0	2	11	0	15	9	.196
Career Totals			**2456**	**8680**	**1074**	**2472**	**483**	**47**	**248**	**1389**	**21**	**855**	**694**	**.285**
STL (13 Yrs)		**NL**	**1564**	**5725**	**736**	**1704**	**332**	**37**	**172**	**929**	**11**	**624**	**453**	**.298**

Getty Images

Larry Walker

Growing up in Canada, Larry Walker had visions of playing in a stadium on ice rather than on grass. Instead of making it with the Montreal Canadians, the five-tool player made it with Montreal Expos and immediately became a national hero. In his fourth season he made his first of five All-Star Game appearances and won the first of seven Gold Glove awards. As the Expos cut costs in 1994, Walker became a free agent and signed with the Colorado Rockies. What became Colorado's gain was Montreal's loss. In the next nine seasons, Walker won a home run title, three batting titles, five Gold Gloves, and an MVP Award. In his 1997 MVP season, Walker drove in 130 runs while batting .366 and stealing 33 bases. His 409 total bases that year rank as the 18th-best total in MLB history—and he kept hitting, batting better than .363 the next two seasons.

His years of success on the field came with many years of injuries. He missed the equivalent of three full seasons due to injuries during his 17-year career, causing one to wonder what his statistics could have been. By 2004 Walker had spent 15 years as one of the game's best but had never played in a World Series. Concerned about his health and salary, the Rockies decided he did not fit into their future and traded him to the division-leading Cardinals in August of that season. Healthy again, he immediately contributed to the Cardinals' pennant run by batting .280 with 11 homers in just 44 games. He then hit .357 with two home runs in the only World Series of his career, in which the Red Sox swept the Redbirds. He spent one more injury-plagued year with the Cardinals before retiring in 2005 and waiting for the call to Cooperstown.

Getty Images

Inducted into the Hall of Fame as a player in 2020 by the BBWAA

Positions: *Right Field, First Base*

Batted: *Left* **Threw:** *Right*

Height: *6' 2"* **Weight:** *185 lbs.*

Born: *December 1, 1966, in Maple Ridge, British Columbia, Canada*

Debut: *August 16, 1989, with the Montreal Expos*

Final game: *October 2, 2005, with the St. Louis Cardinals*

Postseason: *N.L. Pennant (2004)*

Awards & Recognition: *5× All-Star (1992, 1997–1999, 2001), N.L. MVP (1997), 7× Gold Glove Award (1992, 1993, 1997–1999, 2001, 2002), 2× Silver Slugger Award (1992, 1997, 1999), 3× N.L. Batting Leader (1998, 1999, 2001), N.L. Home Run Leader (1997)*

Nickname: *Booger*

Number worn in St. Louis: *Cardinals (33)*

Larry Walker – Career HOF Stats – WAR: 72.7, Slash Line: .313 / .400 / .565

SEASON	TEAM	LG	G	AB	R	H	2B	3B	HR	RBI	SB	BB	SO	BA
1989	MON	NL	20	47	4	8	0	0	0	4	1	5	13	.170
1990	MON	NL	133	419	59	101	18	3	19	51	21	49	112	.241
1991	MON	NL	137	487	59	141	30	2	16	64	14	42	102	.290
1992	MON	NL	143	528	85	159	31	4	23	93	18	41	97	.301
1993	MON	NL	138	490	85	130	24	5	22	86	29	80	76	.265
1994	MON	NL	103	395	76	127	44	2	19	86	15	47	74	.322
1995	COL	NL	131	494	96	151	31	5	36	101	16	49	72	.306
1996	COL	NL	83	272	58	75	18	4	18	58	18	20	58	.276
1997	COL	NL	153	568	143	208	46	4	49	130	33	78	90	.366
1998	COL	NL	130	454	113	165	46	3	23	67	14	64	61	.363
1999	COL	NL	127	438	108	166	26	4	37	115	11	57	52	.379
2000	COL	NL	87	314	64	97	21	7	9	51	5	46	40	.309
2001	COL	NL	142	497	107	174	35	3	38	123	14	82	103	.350
2002	COL	NL	136	477	95	161	40	4	26	104	6	65	73	.338
2003	COL	NL	143	454	86	129	25	7	16	79	7	98	87	.284
2004	COL	NL	38	108	22	35	9	3	6	20	2	25	23	.324
2004	**STL**	**NL**	**44**	**150**	**29**	**42**	**7**	**1**	**11**	**27**	**4**	**24**	**34**	**.280**
2005	**STL**	**NL**	**100**	**315**	**66**	**91**	**20**	**1**	**15**	**52**	**2**	**41**	**64**	**.289**
Career Totals		**NL**	**1988**	**6907**	**1355**	**2160**	**471**	**62**	**383**	**1311**	**230**	**913**	**1231**	**.313**
STL (2 Yrs)		**NL**	**144**	**465**	**95**	**133**	**27**	**2**	**26**	**79**	**6**	**65**	**98**	**.286**

Getty Images

Jim Kaat

Jim Kaat's 25 seasons in the big leagues were spread across four decades. He began his career playing for the Washington Senators in 1959 and went with the team when they relocated to Minnesota in 1961 and became the Twins. Kaat would play for three other teams before ending up in St. Louis in 1980. Those four years with the Cardinals turned out to be his last, but in one sense they were his most fulfilling seasons, because it was as a Cardinal in 1982 that he finally won a World Series Championship ring.

Kaat's Hall of Fame plaque describes the pitcher as an "unwavering workhorse, left-hander won 283 games and pitched 2,540.1 innings." Fourteen times during that career he pitched more than 200 innings in a season. Twice in that run he exceeded three hundred innings in a season. Using a masterful quick-pitch delivery, the three-time All-Star became a defensive wizard, accumulating 16 straight gold gloves (1962–1977).

For 13 seasons Kaat anchored the Twins rotation, including in 1965, when they won the A.L. pennant only to lose in the World Series to the Los Angeles Dodgers in seven games. Kaat pitched in three games in that Series, going 1–2. At age 40 in 1979 Kaat made the transition from being one of the game's best starters to being a steady lefty out of the bullpen with the Yankees. The next year Kaat was sold to the Cardinals to both start and relieve. Although he only started two games in the team's 1982 World Championship season, Kaat was used in 60 other games as a lefthanded setup reliever before Bruce Sutter's entry to close out the game. Kaat relieved in four games that Series and began the following season with the Redbirds before being released in July 1983. Upon his retirement, Kaat had accumulated the most MLB seasons of any pitcher in the history of the game and wound up ranking sixth for the most games ever started.

Inducted into the Hall of Fame as a player in 2022 by the Golden Days Era Committee

Position: *Pitcher*

Batted: *Left* **Threw:** *Left*

Height: *6' 4"* **Weight:** *205 lbs.*

Born: *November 7, 1938, in Zeeland, MI*

Debut: *August 2, 1959, with the Washington Senators*

Final game: *July 1, 1983, with the St. Louis Cardinals*

Postseason: *World Series Champion (1982), A.L. Pennant (1965), N.L. Pennant (1982)*

Awards & Recognition: *3× All-Star (1962, 1966, 1975), 16× Gold Glove Award (1962–1977), A.L. Wins Leader (1966)*

Nickname: *Kitty*

Number worn in St. Louis: *Cardinals (36)*

Jim Kaat – Career HOF Stats – WAR: 50.5

YEAR(S)	SEASONS	TEAM	LEAGUE	W	L	ERA	G	CG	SHO	SV	IP	H	HR	BB	SO
1959 - 1973	15	WSH / MIN	AL	190	159	3.34	484	133	23	5	3014.1	2982	279	729	1851
1973 - 1975	3	CHW	Al	45	28	3.10	92	30	5	0	623.2	628	42	144	300
1976 - 1979	4	PHI	NL	27	30	4.23	102	11	2	0	536.2	611	51	109	188
1979 - 1980	2	NYY	AL	2	4	4.12	44	0	0	2	63.1	72	4	18	24
1980 - 1983	**4**	**STL**	**NL**	**19**	**16**	**3.82**	**176**	**6**	**1**	**10**	**292.1**	**327**	**19**	**83**	**98**
Career Totals	**25**			**283**	**237**	**3.450**	**898**	**180**	**31**	**17**	**4530.1**	**4620**	**395**	**1083**	**2461**

Getty Images

Minnie Miñoso

For over five decades Orestes Miñoso was known simply as "Minnie," a nickname that originated in Cleveland and not in his native Cuba, where he had become a standout player. His rise in baseball from Cuba to America's Negro Leagues and then the Hall of Fame became an inspiration for young Latino boys playing the game. He would become Major League Baseball's first Latin superstar. In his autobiography Orlando Cepeda wrote: "Minnie Miñoso is to Latin ballplayers what Jackie Robinson is to Black ballplayers."

Miñoso spent 17 seasons in the majors playing for four teams over a span of five decades. He joined the Cleveland Indians in 1949 as a two-time Negro League All Star. He made the Indians' roster without ever playing in the minors and walked in his pinch-hit debut on April 19 against the St. Louis Browns. Unable to crack the Indians' lineup, Miñoso was traded to the White Sox in 1951. He became a nine-time All-Star and a regular A.L. leader in hit-by-pitches, triples, and stolen bases. He exceeded the 100 mark multiple times for runs scored and RBIs and was an inaugural winner of Major League Baseball's Gold Glove Award playing left field in 1957.

He missed the Sox's 1959 World Series after a trade to Cleveland and was traded again to the Cardinals in 1962 as they sought a veteran outfielder. Miñoso only played 39 games with the Redbirds after running into the wall at Sportsman's Park, fracturing his skull and breaking his wrist. Sold to the Senators after the season, he retired in 1964. In 1976 while Miñoso was coaching the Sox, Bill Veeck activated him for three games, and he got a hit playing in his fourth decade. In 1980, at the age of 56, he was activated once more for two games and two at bats (no hits) in his fifth decade in the big leagues.

Wikimedia Commons

Inducted into the Hall of Fame in as a player in 2022 by the Golden Days Era Committee

Positions: *Left Field, Third Base*

Batted: *Right* **Threw:** *Right*

Height: *5' 10"* **Weight:** *175 lbs.*

Born: *November 28, 1924, in Perico, Cuba*

Died: *March 1, 2015, in Chicago, IL*

Buried: *Graceland Cemetery, Chicago, IL*

Debut: *April 19, 1949, with the Cleveland Indians*

Final game: *October 5, 1980, with the Chicago White Sox*

Postseason: *Negro World Series Champion (1947)*

Awards & Recognition: *2× Negro League All-Star (1947, 1948), 9× MLB All-Star (1951–1954, 1957, 1959–1960), 3× Gold Glove Award (1957, 1959, 1960), 3× A.L. Stolen Base Leader (1951–1953)*

Number worn in St. Louis: *Cardinals (9)*

Minnie Miñoso – HOF Career Playing Stats – WAR: 53.3, Slash Line: .299 / .387 / .461

SEASON	TEAM	LG	G	AB	R	H	2B	3B	HR	RBI	SB	BB	SO	BA
1946	NYC	NN2	37	146	23	33	5	2	4	14	1	13		.226
1947	NYC	NN2	40	177	42	63	13	4	2	25	5	13		.356
1948	NYC	NN2	36	157	27	54	11	6	3	27	5	8		.344
1949	CLE	AL	9	16	2	3	0	0	1	1	0	2	2	.188
1951	CLE	AL	8	14	3	6	2	0	0	2	0	1	1	.429
1951	CHW	AL	138	516	109	167	32	14	10	74	31	71	41	.324
1952	CHW	AL	147	569	96	160	24	9	13	61	22	71	46	.281
1953	CHW	AL	151	556	104	174	24	8	15	104	25	74	43	.313
1954	CHW	AL	153	568	119	182	29	18	19	116	18	77	46	.320
1955	CHW	AL	139	517	79	149	26	7	10	70	19	76	43	.288
1956	CHW	AL	151	545	106	172	29	11	21	88	12	86	40	.316
1957	CHW	AL	153	568	96	176	36	5	12	103	18	79	54	.310
1958	CLE	AL	149	556	94	168	25	2	24	80	14	59	53	.302
1959	CLE	AL	148	570	92	172	32	0	21	92	8	54	46	.302
1960	CHW	AL	154	591	89	184	32	4	20	105	17	52	63	.311
1961	CHW	AL	152	540	91	151	28	3	14	82	9	67	46	.280
1962	**STL**	**NL**	**39**	**97**	**14**	**19**	**5**	**0**	**1**	**10**	**4**	**7**	**17**	**.196**
1963	WSA	AL	109	315	38	72	12	2	4	30	8	33	38	.229
1964	CHW	AL	30	31	4	7	0	0	1	5	0	5	3	.226
1976	CHW	AL	3	8	0	1	0	0	0	0	0	0	2	.125
1980	CHW	AL	2	2	0	0	0	0	0	0	0	0	0	.000
Career Totals			**1948**	**7059**	**1228**	**2113**	**365**	**95**	**195**	**1089**	**216**	**848**	**584**	**.299**

Getty Images

Scott Rolen

For many fans Brooks Robinson, Mike Schmidt, and Scott Rolen are the Mount Rushmore of third basemen. Rolen's Hall of Fame plaque states he "paired elite glovework with a formidable bat to become a dominant two-way threat." What might his numbers have been had he not been plagued by injuries? In his 17 big league seasons, Rolen played 100 or fewer games seven times.

But when he played, he played the right way, as noted by teammate Jonny Gomes: "You know 'W.W.J.D., what would Jesus do'? Here, it's what would Scott do? He doesn't argue with the umpires, he runs every single ball out, he makes great plays, he makes routine plays, he gets the runner in when he needs to get him in, he gets the runner over when he needs to get him over. He just plays the game exactly how it should be played. You never second-guess anything he does."

Rolen did it right from the very start as a unanimous Rookie of the Year Award winner with the Philadelphia Phillies in 1997. He became a seven-time All-Star while collecting eight Gold Gloves. He retired as one of only three third basemen with 300 home runs, 500 doubles, and 100 stolen bases. But he never made the playoffs during his seven seasons in Philadelphia and questioned whether they would spend the money to get there. In 2002 he was traded to the Cardinals and was in the playoffs and soon the World Series. His postseason hitting contributions are etched in Cardinal postseason lore. His go-ahead home run off Roger Clemens in Game Seven of the 2004 NLCS launched Rolen into his first World Series, and his Game One shot off Jason Verlander in the 2006 Series set the stage for the Cardinals and Rolen to become World Champions.

Inducted into the Hall of Fame as a player in 2023 by the BBWAA

Position: *Third Base*

Batted: *Right* **Threw:** *Right*

Height: *6' 4"* **Weight:** *245 lbs.*

Born: *April 4, 1975, in Evansville, IN*

Debut: *August 1, 1996, with the Philadelphia Phillies*

Final game: *October 3, 2012, with the Cincinnati Reds*

Postseason: *1x World Series Champion (2006), 2x N.L. Pennant (2004, 2006)*

Awards & Recognition: *7× All-Star (2002–2006, 2010, 2011), N.L. Rookie of the Year (1997), 8× Gold Glove Award (1998, 2000–2004, 2006, 2010), Silver Slugger Award (2002)*

Number(s) worn in St. Louis: *Cardinals (16, 27)*

Scott Rolen – HOF Career Stats – WAR: 70.1, Slash Line: .281 / .364 / .490

SEASON	TEAM	LG	G	AB	R	H	2B	3B	HR	RBI	SB	BB	SO	BA
1996	PHI	NL	37	130	10	33	7	0	4	18	0	13	27	.254
1997	PHI	NL	156	561	93	159	35	3	21	92	16	76	138	.283
1998	PHI	NL	160	601	120	174	45	4	31	110	14	93	141	.290
1999	PHI	NL	112	421	74	113	28	1	26	77	12	67	114	.268
2000	PHI	NL	128	483	88	144	32	6	26	89	8	51	99	.298
2001	PHI	NL	151	554	96	160	39	1	25	107	16	74	127	.289
2002	PHI	NL	100	375	52	97	21	4	17	66	5	52	68	.259
2002	**STL**	**NL**	**55**	**205**	**37**	**57**	**8**	**4**	**14**	**44**	**3**	**20**	**34**	**.278**
2003	**STL**	**NL**	**154**	**559**	**98**	**160**	**49**	**1**	**28**	**104**	**13**	**82**	**104**	**.286**
2004	**STL**	**NL**	**142**	**500**	**109**	**157**	**32**	**4**	**34**	**124**	**4**	**72**	**92**	**.314**
2005	**STL**	**NL**	**56**	**196**	**28**	**46**	**12**	**1**	**5**	**28**	**1**	**25**	**28**	**.235**
2006	**STL**	**NL**	**142**	**521**	**94**	**154**	**48**	**1**	**22**	**95**	**7**	**56**	**69**	**.296**
2007	**STL**	**NL**	**112**	**392**	**55**	**104**	**24**	**2**	**8**	**58**	**5**	**37**	**56**	**.265**
2008	TOR	AL	115	408	58	107	30	3	11	50	5	46	71	.262
2009	TOR	AL	88	338	52	108	29	0	8	43	4	26	42	.320
2009	CIN	NL	40	137	24	37	7	1	3	24	1	19	20	.270
2010	CIN	NL	133	471	66	134	34	3	20	83	1	50	82	.285
2011	CIN	NL	65	252	31	61	20	2	5	36	1	10	36	.242
2012	CIN	NL	92	294	26	72	17	2	8	39	2	30	62	.245
Career Totals			**2038**	**7398**	**1211**	**2077**	**517**	**43**	**316**	**1287**	**118**	**899**	**1410**	**.281**
STL (6 Yrs)		**NL**	**661**	**2373**	**421**	**678**	**173**	**13**	**111**	**453**	**33**	**292**	**383**	**.286**

Getty Images

Dick Allen

During his 1964 Rookie of the Year award winning season, Dick Allen established himself as one of baseball's most feared hitters of the 1960s and early 1970s. It was one of baseball's best rookie seasons ever. Allen led the N.L. in runs (125), triples (13), extra base hits (80), and total bases (352); while also finishing in the top five in batting average (.318), slugging average (.557), hits (201), and doubles (38). He nearly single-handedly lifted the Phillies to the N.L. pennant. But the Phillies lost 10 of their final 12 games and blew a 6 ½ game lead, allowing the Cardinals to win the pennant. It wasn't Allen's fault. He hit .438 with 5 doubles, 2 triples, 3 home runs and 11 RBI during those final 12 games.

Allen hit his way to three All-Star appearances in Philadelphia before being packaged in a seven-player trade to St. Louis in 1970 that included Curt Flood and Tim McCarver. It was the trade that led to Flood's eventual Supreme Court challenge of baseball's reserve clause. In St. Louis Allen had another All-Star season, hitting 34 home runs and collecting 101 RBIs in an injury-shortened 122 games. In somewhat of a surprise move the Cardinals traded Allen to the Dodgers for Ted Sizemore and Bob Stinson. The Cardinals rationalized the trade as a need to find a replacement for an aging Julián Javier at second base.

Allen had another quality season with the Dodgers in 1971, but he wasn't in sync with the team ownership's off-field demands and was shipped off to the White Sox. Allen's seasons in Chicago helped revitalize baseball on the city's South Side. His three All-Star seasons made the team a pennant contender. In 1972 Allen led the A.L. in Home Runs and RBI but fell just short of a Triple Crown season when his .308 batting average ranked third in the league. He did, however, wind up winning the A.L. MVP Award.

Getty Images

Inducted into the Hall of Fame as a player in 2025 by the Classic Baseball Era Committee

Positions: *First Base, Third Base and Leftfield*

Batted: *Right* **Threw:** *Right*

Height: *5' 11"* **Weight:** *187 lbs.*

Born: *March 8, 1942, in Wampum, PA*

Died: *December 7, 2020, in Wampum, PA*

Buried: *Clinton Cemetery, Wampum, PA*

Debut: *September 3, 1963, with the Philadelphia Phillies*

Final Game: *June 19, 1977, with the Oakland A's*

Nicknames: *Wampum Walloper, Richie or Crash*

Postseason: *NA*

Awards & Recognition: *7× All-Star (1965–1967, 1970, 1972–1974) NL Rookie of the Year (1964), A.L. MVP (1972), 2× A.L. home run leader (1972, 1974), A.L. RBI leader (1972)*

Number(s) worn in St. Louis: *Cardinals (15)*

Dick Allen – Career Playing Stats – WAR: 58.7, Slash Line: .292 / .378 / .534

YEAR(S)	TEAM	LEAGUE	G	AB	R	H	2B	3B	HR	RBI	SB	BB	SO	BA
1963	PHI	NL	10	24	6	7	2	1	0	2	0	0	5	.292
1964	PHI	NL	162	632	125	201	38	13	29	91	3	67	138	.318
1965	PHI	NL	161	619	93	187	31	14	20	85	15	74	150	.302
1966	PHI	NL	141	524	112	166	25	10	40	110	10	68	136	.317
1967	PHI	NL	122	463	89	142	31	10	23	77	20	75	117	.307
1968	PHI	NL	152	521	87	137	17	9	33	90	7	74	161	.263
1969	PHI	NL	118	438	79	126	23	3	32	89	9	64	144	.288
1970	**STL**	**NL**	**122**	**459**	**88**	**128**	**17**	**5**	**34**	**101**	**5**	**71**	**118**	**.279**
1971	LAD	NL	155	549	82	162	24	1	23	90	8	93	113	.295
1972	CHW	AL	148	506	90	156	28	5	37	113	19	99	126	.308
1973	CHW	AL	72	250	39	79	20	3	16	41	7	33	51	.316
1974	CHW	AL	128	462	84	139	23	1	32	88	7	57	89	.301
1975	PHI	NL	119	416	54	97	21	3	12	62	11	58	109	.233
1976	PHI	NL	85	298	52	80	16	1	15	49	11	37	63	.268
1977	OAK	AL	54	171	19	41	4	0	5	31	1	24	36	.240
Career Totals			**1749**	**6332**	**1099**	**1848**	**320**	**79**	**351**	**1119**	**133**	**894**	**1556**	**.292**

Getty Images

All images: St. Louis Browns Historical Society

Missouri Historical Society, St. Louis

St. Louis Browns Historical Society

Players from the St. Louis Browns Franchise

The St. Louis Browns were an American League team that played in St. Louis between 1902 and 1953. They were not an original member of the American League when it was formed in 1901. But St. Louis was America's fourth-largest city then, with a rich baseball history dating back to the city's first professional game in July 1860 at Fairground Park between the Cyclones and the Morning Stars. In 1901 the Cardinals were a floundering franchise, usually finishing last or near last in the National League standings. In the league's second season, American League president Ban Johnson decided to move the Milwaukee Brewers to St. Louis hoping his league's team would flourish and win over St. Louis's baseball-loving fans—something the Browns did during their first two decades in St. Louis.

Upon moving to St. Louis from Milwaukee, the team adopted the Browns moniker in recognition of earlier teams playing under that name within St. Louis's long baseball history. Fate would throw the franchise multiple curve balls both on and off the field, leading to St. Louis being branded as "First in Booze, First in Shoes, and Last in the American League." The bottom line is that the Browns were seldom winners, managing only one American League pennant in their 52-year history compared to the Cardinals' 19 pennants and 11 World Championships. Winners take it all, and the Browns could never keep up with their N.L. city-mates. Following the 1953 season, the franchise moved and became the Baltimore Orioles.

Even though they weren't always winners, the Browns had many great players, including one who ranks as one of the best ever to play the game. The following pages tell the story of those Hall of Fame inductees who spent time with the St. Louis Browns. This section does not include the six additional Hall of Fame inductees with ties to the team (Bottomley, Burkett, Dean, Hornsby, Rickey, and Wallace) who are included within the Cardinals pages since they spent more time as Redbirds than as members of the Browns.

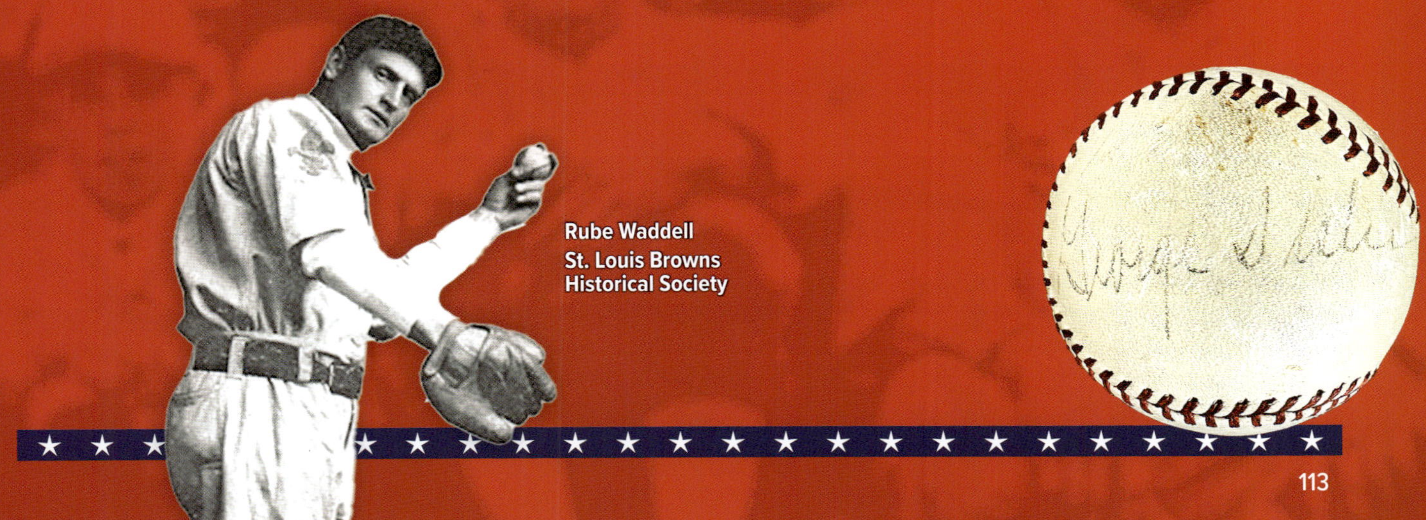

Rube Waddell
St. Louis Browns Historical Society

George Sisler

George Sisler was one of baseball's first superstars, yet his career with the St. Louis Browns is as forgotten as the legacy of the team on which he starred. Had it not been for his hitting records being topped with great fanfare by Ichiro Suzuki in October 2004, today's fans may have never heard of the man who was called "Gorgeous George." If the saying "it takes one to know one" is true, Ty Cobb's description of Sisler as "the nearest thing to a perfect ballplayer" he had ever seen clearly sums it up.

Sisler began his career as a pitcher and became one of the game's first great "five-tool" players. Sisler's move from pitcher to an everyday first baseman to take advantage of his offensive prowess mirrors Babe Ruth's move from pitching to the outfield for the same reason. While not having the home run numbers of Lou Gehrig, Sisler is usually considered the better of the two at first base defensively. Sisler was also the better hitter for average as opposed to power. He hit .407 in 1920 and .420 in 1922. With an average of .371 sandwiched in between in 1921, his three-year batting average topped the .400 mark. Getting on base is the key to scoring, and Sisler stroked over 200 hits six times, including his record-setting 257 hits played within the 154-game schedule of 1920—a record topped by Ichiro's 262 hits in 2004 while batting .372 in 161 games.

Sisler was also a skilled baserunner and led the A.L. four times in stolen bases. Today he remains the Browns/Orioles franchise career leader in stolen bases and triples. For three seasons Sisler also managed the Browns, but few remember that George Sisler was awarded baseball's first Most Valuable Player Award in 1922. So as not to forget the St. Louis Browns and one of their players who was one of the best in the game, the St. Louis Cardinals have erected a bronze statue of Sisler within their ring of Cardinals Hall of Famers' statues outside Busch Stadium III.

Library of Congress

Inducted into the Hall of Fame as a player in 1939 by the BBWAA

Positions: *First Base, Manager*

Batted: *Left* **Threw:** *Left*

Height: *5' 11"* **Weight:** *170 lbs.*

Born: *March 24, 1893, in Manchester, OH*

Died: *March 26, 1973, in Richmond Heights, MO*

Buried: *Old Meeting House Presbyterian Church Cemetery, Frontenac, MO*

Debut: *June 28, 1915, with the St. Louis Browns*

Final game: *September 22, 1930, with the Boston Braves*

Postseason: *N/A*

Awards & Recognition: *MLB MVP (1922), 2× A.L. Batting Leader (1920, 1922), 4× A.L. Stolen Base Leader (1918, 1921, 1922, 1927)*

Nickname: *Gorgeous George*

Number worn in St. Louis: *Played prior to numbers being worn*

George Sisler – Career Managerial Stats

YEAR(S)	SEASONS	TEAM	LEAGUE	WON	LOST	W-L%	TIES	GAMES	EJECTIONS	PENNANTS	CHAMPIONSHIPS
1924 - 1926	3	SLB	AL	218	241	.475	3	462	3	0	0
Career Totals	**3**	**SLB**	**AL**	**218**	**241**	**.475**	**3**	**462**	**3**	**0**	**0**

George Sisler – HOF Career Playing Stats – WAR: 57.2, Slash Line: .340 / .379 / .468

YEAR(S)	SEASONS	TEAM	LEAGUE	G	AB	R	H	2B	3B	HR	RBI	SB	BB	SO	BA
1915 - 1922, 1924 - 1927	12	SLB	AL	1647	6667	1091	2295	343	145	93	962	351	385	278	.344
1928	1	WSH	AL	20	49	1	12	1	0	0	2	0	1	2	.245
1928 - 1930	3	BSN	NL	388	1551	192	505	81	19	9	214	24	86	47	.326
Career Totals	**15**			**2055**	**8267**	**1284**	**2812**	**425**	**164**	**102**	**1178.0**	**375**	**472**	**327**	**.340**

Library of Congress

Eddie Plank

For 17 seasons Eddie Plank was baseball's preeminent lefthanded pitcher. He was the first lefthander to win 300 games and retired having won 326 games—a mark that now ranks third for southpaws and 13th overall. His 305 wins in the A.L. are still tops by a lefty in that league. It took 42 years after he retired in 1917 to have Plank's major league wins record as a southpaw topped by Warren Spahn in 1962. He was the A.L.'s winningest pitcher (left- or right-handed) until 1921 when Walter Johnson topped Plank's total.

Plank won 284 games with the Philadelphia Athletics between 1901 and 1914. He played on five pennant-winning teams and won three World Championships. After the A's won four pennants in the five seasons between 1910 and 1914, owner Connie Mack decided to break up the team and Plank was released in the shake-up.

After 15 seasons and with the end of his career looming, Plank signed with the St. Louis Terriers of the "Outlaw" Federal League in 1915. The end was not that near for Eddie as he won 21 games for the Terriers that year. It was, however, the end for the Federal League after just two years as a rival to the A.L and N.L. After the league's demise Terrier owner Phil Ball took ownership of the A.L.'s St. Louis Browns and signed the 40-year-old Plank to his new A.L. team. The 16 wins Plank had for the Browns in 1916 were immortalized in one of sports-writing great Grantland Rice's memorable poems: "Drift on, old top, and hold the track that echoes with resounding cheers / with fate and time both driven back I hope you last for ninety years!" Plank barely got through the following season, posting a 5–6 record before calling it quits as one of the game's best ever.

Library of Congress

Inducted into the Hall of Fame as a player in 1946 by the Old Timers Committee

Position: *Pitcher*

Batted: *Left* **Threw:** *Left*

Height: *5' 11"* **Weight:** *175 lbs.*

Born: *August 31, 1875, in Gettysburg, PA*

Died: *February 24, 1925, in Gettysburg, PA*

Buried: *Evergreen Cemetery, Gettysburg, PA*

Debut: *May 31, 1901, with the Philadelphia Athletics*

Final game: *August 6, 1917, with the St. Louis Browns*

Postseason: *3× World Series Champion (1910, 1911, 1913), 5× A.L. Pennant (1905, 1910, 1911, 1913, 1914)*

Awards & Recognition: *N/A*

Nickname: *Gettysburg Eddie*

Number worn in St. Louis: *Played prior to numbers being worn*

Eddie Plank Career HOF Stats – WAR: 90.9

YEAR	TEAM	LG	W	L	ERA	G	CG	SHO	SV	IP	H	HR	BB	SO
1901	PHA	AL	17	13	3.31	33	28	1	0	260.2	254	3	68	90
1902	PHA	AL	20	15	3.30	36	31	1	0	300	319	5	61	107
1903	PHA	AL	23	16	2.38	43	33	3	0	336	317	5	65	176
1904	PHA	AL	26	17	2.17	44	37	7	0	357.1	311	2	86	201
1905	PHA	AL	24	12	2.26	41	35	4	0	346.2	287	3	75	210
1906	PHA	AL	19	6	2.25	26	21	5	0	211.2	173	1	51	108
1907	PHA	AL	24	16	2.20	43	33	8	0	343.2	282	5	85	183
1908	PHA	AL	14	16	2.17	34	21	4	1	244.2	202	1	46	135
1909	PHA	AL	19	10	1.76	34	24	3	0	265.1	215	1	62	132
1910	PHA	AL	16	10	2.01	38	22	1	2	250.1	218	3	55	123
1911	PHA	AL	23	8	2.10	40	24	6	4	256.2	237	2	77	149
1912	PHA	AL	26	6	2.22	37	23	5	2	259.2	234	1	83	110
1913	PHA	AL	18	10	2.60	41	18	7	4	242.2	211	3	57	151
1914	PHA	AL	15	7	2.87	34	12	4	3	185.1	178	2	42	110
1915	SLM	FL	21	11	2.08	42	23	6	3	268.1	212	1	54	147
1916	SLB	AL	16	15	2.33	37	17	3	3	235.2	203	2	67	88
1917	SLB	AL	5	6	1.79	20	8	1	1	131	105	2	38	26
Career Totals			326	194	2.35	623	410	69	23	4495.2	3958	42	1072	2246
SLB (2 yrs)		AL	21	21	2.14	57	25	4	4	366.2	308	4	105	114
SLM (1 yr)		FL	21	11	2.08	42	23	6	3	268.1	212	1	54	147

Library of Congress

Rube Waddell

The very eccentric George Waddell was given the moniker "Rube" due to his larger size and innocent ways. On the mound he could be a dominating pitcher; he was described by his manager Connie Mack as having "more stuff than any pitcher I ever saw." Off the mound his childlike ways often made him easily distracted and unpredictable. On impulse Waddell would leave a game to go fishing or could be found wrestling alligators. Baseball gave him purpose. He joined the N.L.'s Louisville Colonels in 1897 and bounced around the league for several years with several teams posting mediocre results. He was found by Connie Mack, who brought the lefthander to the Philadelphia Athletics in 1902. Under Mack's tutelage, Waddell posted four straight seasons of 20 or more wins and led the majors in strikeouts six straight years while averaging 262 whiffs per season. Twice he fanned more than 300 hitters. In 1905 he won the pitching triple crown, leading the A.L. in wins (27), strikeouts (287), and ERA (1.48). How good was Waddell? Walter Johnson declared, "In my opinion, Rube Waddell had more sheer pitching ability than any man I ever saw."

Tired of Waddell's antics, at times induced by his heavy drinking, Mack sold Waddell to the St. Louis Browns in 1908. His 19 wins pushed the Browns into the A.L.'s upper division that year and improved their attendance. He even tied a baseball record by striking out 16 of his former A's teammates. By the next year, Waddell was no longer the pitcher he had been, finishing the season with more losses than wins. He would begin his last season in 1910 and would play in only 10 games with the Browns to end his 13-season career in the big leagues.

Library of Congress

Inducted into the Hall of Fame as a player in 1946 by the Old Timers Committee

Position: *Pitcher*

Batted: *Right* **Threw:** *Left*

Height: *6' 1"* **Weight:** *196 lbs.*

Born: *October 12, 1876, in Bradford, PA*

Died: *April 1, 1941, in Elmendorf, TX*

Buried: *Mission Burial Park South, San Antonio, TX*

Debut: *September 8, 1897, with the Louisville Colonels*

Final game: *August 1, 1910, with the St. Louis Browns*

Postseason: *A.L. Pennant—but did not pitch (1905)*

Awards & Recognition: *Pitching Triple Crown (1905), A.L. Wins Leader (1905), 2× A.L. ERA Leader (1900, 1905), 6× A.L. Strikeout Leader (1902–1907)*

Nickname: *Rube*

Number worn in St. Louis: *Played prior to numbers being worn*

Rube Waddell – HOF Career Pitching Stats – WAR: 58.4

YEAR	TEAM	LG	W	L	ERA	G	CG	SHO	SV	IP	H	HR	BB	SO
1897	LOU	NL	0	1	3.21	2	1	0	0	14	17	0	6	5
1899	LOU	NL	7	2	3.08	10	9	1	1	79	69	4	14	44
1900	PIT	NL	8	13	2.37	29	16	2	0	208.2	176	3	55	130
1901	TOT	NL	14	16	3.01	31	26	0	0	251.1	249	5	75	172
1901	PIT	NL	0	2	9.39	2	0	0	0	7.2	10	0	9	4
1901	CHC	NL	14	14	2.81	29	26	0	0	243.2	239	5	66	168
1902	PHA	AL	24	7	2.05	33	26	3	0	276.1	224	7	64	210
1903	PHA	AL	21	16	2.44	39	34	4	0	324	274	3	85	302
1904	PHA	AL	25	19	1.62	46	39	8	0	383	307	5	91	349
1905	PHA	AL	27	10	1.48	46	27	7	0	328.2	231	5	90	287
1906	PHA	AL	15	17	2.21	43	22	8	0	272.2	221	1	92	196
1907	PHA	AL	19	13	2.15	44	20	7	0	284.2	234	2	73	232
1908	**SLB**	**AL**	**19**	**14**	**1.89**	**43**	**25**	**5**	**3**	**285.2**	**223**	**0**	**90**	**232**
1909	**SLB**	**AL**	**11**	**14**	**2.37**	**31**	**16**	**5**	**0**	**220.1**	**204**	**1**	**57**	**141**
1910	**SLB**	**AL**	**3**	**1**	**3.55**	**10**	**0**	**0**	**1**	**33**	**31**	**1**	**11**	**16**
Career Totals			193	143	2.16	407	261	50	5	2961.1	2460	37	803	2316
SLB (3 yrs)		**AL**	**33**	**29**	**2.19**	**84**	**41**	**10**	**4**	**539**	**458**	**2**	**158**	**389**

Missouri Historical Society, St. Louis

Heinie Manush

Henry (Heinie) Manush was one of baseball's best hitters during the 1920s and 1930s. He played for six teams during his 17 seasons in the majors, including two and a half seasons with the St. Louis Browns (1928–1930). Manush broke into the big leagues with the Detroit Tigers in 1923 and became an offensive force, batting .334 in his rookie season and three seasons later leading the A.L with a .378 average. Despite his success, Detroit included Manush in a postseason trade to the St. Louis Browns in 1927.

Playing in all 154 games in 1928, Manush missed winning his second batting title on the last day of the season when the Washington Senators' Goose Goslin singled against the Browns during his final at bat that year to end the season with a .379 batting average to Manush's .378. Although Manush didn't win the batting title, he led the majors in hits and the A.L. in doubles. That season only Babe Ruth had more total bases and only Ruth and Lou Gehrig had more extra base hits than Manush. He would again lead the league in doubles the following season with the Browns and finish second in the MVP race for the second year in a row.

Although he hit .328 in 1930 Manush had fallen from favor with the Browns by holding out for more money that spring. In Washington, the man who had beaten Manush for the 1928 batting title had also fallen out of favor with management. In mid-June both players were included in a trade between the Browns and Senators. Offensively, there wouldn't be much difference in either hitters' production numbers. But the real difference after the trade was that Washington had the better team, allowing Manush to play in his only World Series in 1933.

Wikimedia Commons

Inducted into the Hall of Fame as a player in 1964 by the Veterans Committee

Position: *Left field*

Batted: *Left* **Threw:** *Left*

Height: *6' 1"* **Weight:** *200 lbs.*

Born: *July 29, 1901, in Tuscumbia, AL*

Died: *May 12, 1971, in Sarasota, FL*

Buried: *Sarasota Memorial Park, Sarasota, FL*

Debut: *April 20, 1923, with the Detroit Tigers*

Final game: *May 22, 1939, with the Pittsburgh Pirates*

Postseason: *A.L. Pennant (1933)*

Awards & Recognition: *All-Star (1934), A.L. Batting Leader (1926)*

Number worn in St. Louis: *Played prior to numbers being worn*

Heinie Manush HOF Career Playing Stats – WAR: 48.1, Slash Line: .330 / .377 / .479

SEASON	TEAM	LG	G	AB	R	H	2B	3B	HR	RBI	SB	BB	SO	BA
1923	DET	AL	109	308	59	103	20	5	4	54	3	20	21	.334
1924	DET	AL	120	422	84	122	24	8	9	68	14	27	30	.289
1925	DET	AL	99	278	47	84	14	3	5	47	8	24	21	.302
1926	DET	AL	136	498	95	188	35	8	14	86	11	31	28	.378
1927	DET	AL	151	593	101	177	31	18	6	90	12	47	29	.298
1928	**SLB**	**AL**	**154**	**638**	**104**	**241**	**47**	**20**	**13**	**108**	**16**	**39**	**14**	**.378**
1929	**SLB**	**AL**	**142**	**574**	**85**	**204**	**45**	**10**	**6**	**81**	**9**	**43**	**24**	**.355**
1930	**SLB**	**AL**	**49**	**198**	**26**	**65**	**16**	**4**	**2**	**29**	**3**	**5**	**7**	**.328**
1930	WSH	AL	88	356	74	129	33	8	7	65	4	26	17	.362
1931	WSH	AL	146	616	110	189	41	11	6	70	3	36	27	.307
1932	WSH	AL	149	625	121	214	41	14	14	116	7	36	29	.342
1933	WSH	AL	153	658	115	221	32	17	5	95	6	36	18	.336
1934	WSH	AL	137	556	88	194	42	11	11	89	7	36	23	.349
1935	WSH	AL	119	479	68	131	26	9	4	56	2	35	17	.273
1936	BOS	AL	82	313	43	91	15	5	0	45	1	17	11	.291
1937	BRO	NL	132	466	57	155	25	7	4	73	6	40	24	.333
1938	2TM	NL	32	64	11	16	4	2	0	10	1	7	4	.250
1938	BRO	NL	17	51	9	12	3	1	0	6	1	5	4	.235
1938	PIT	NL	15	13	2	4	1	1	0	4	0	2	0	.308
1939	PIT	NL	10	12	0	0	0	0	0	1	0	1	1	.000
Career Totals			**2008**	**7654**	**1288**	**2524**	**491**	**160**	**110**	**1183**	**113**	**506**	**345**	**.330**
SLB (3 Yrs)		**AL**	**345**	**1410**	**215**	**510**	**108**	**34**	**21**	**218**	**28**	**87**	**45**	**.362**

Library of Congress

Goose Goslin

Leon Allen "Goose" Goslin played for three big league teams over an 18-year career that included three seasons with the St. Louis Browns (1930–1932). Goslin was an All-Star only once in his career (1936) because the Midseason Classic didn't begin until 1933. Goslin broke into the majors with the Washington Senators in 1921, having been christened with the nickname "Goose" because of the way he flapped his arms while chasing balls. The nickname inspired sportswriter W.O. McGeehan to write that "for the country at large the eagle may remain the national bird, but for the National Capital the greatest bird that flies is the Goose." Goslin went on to become one of the franchise's best offensive players.

He hit .324 in his first full season with the Senators in 1922 and would top the .300 mark the next six seasons, leading the A.L. with his .379 batting title win over the Browns' Heine Manush in 1928. Goslin won it with a hit in his last at bat in the last game of the season. Goslin's offense, along with Walter Johnson's pitching, helped spark the Senators to two consecutive World Series appearances in 1924 and 1925. Their win in 1924 would be the only World Championship won by the franchise in the nation's capital.

In June 1930 the Senators traded Goslin to the Browns for batting rival Heine Manush. Goslin responded to the trade with power, adding 30 home runs in St. Louis to the seven he had hit up to that point in the season in Washington for a new career mark. In 1932, Goslin tried using a bat that featured 12 longitudinal green stripes while with the Browns. The umpire wouldn't allow it, and subsequently the league deemed the "zebra bat" illegal as it could be a distraction to fielders.

Library of Congress

Inducted into the Hall of Fame as a player in 1968 by the Veterans Committee

Position: *Left Field*

Batted: *Left* **Threw:** *Right*

Height: *5' 11"* **Weight:** *185 lbs.*

Born: *October 16, 1900, in Salem, NJ*

Died: *May 15, 1971, in Bridgeton, NJ*

Buried: *Baptist Cemetery, Salem, NJ*

Debut: *September 16, 1921, with the Washington Senators*

Final game: *September 23, 1938, with the Washington Senators*

Postseason: *2× World Series Champion (1924, 1935), 5× A.L. Pennant (1924, 1925, 1933, 1934, 1935)*

Awards & Recognition: *All-Star (1936), A.L. Batting Leader (1928), A.L. RBI Leader (1924)*

Nickname: *Goose*

Number worn in St. Louis: *Browns (3)*

Goose Goslin – HOF Career Playing Stats – WAR: 66.0, Slash Line: .316 / .387 / .500

SEASON	TEAM	LG	G	AB	R	H	2B	3B	HR	RBI	SB	BB	SO	BA
1921	WSH	AL	14	50	8	13	1	1	1	6	0	6	5	.260
1922	WSH	AL	101	358	44	116	19	7	3	53	4	25	26	.324
1923	WSH	AL	150	600	86	180	29	18	9	99	7	40	53	.300
1924	WSH	AL	154	579	100	199	30	17	12	129	15	68	29	.344
1925	WSH	AL	150	601	116	201	34	20	18	113	27	53	50	.334
1926	WSH	AL	147	568	105	201	26	15	17	109	8	63	38	.354
1927	WSH	AL	148	581	96	194	37	15	13	120	21	50	28	.334
1928	WSH	AL	135	456	80	173	36	10	17	102	16	48	19	.379
1929	WSH	AL	145	553	82	159	28	7	18	91	11	66	33	.288
1930	2TM	AL	148	584	115	180	36	12	37	138	17	67	54	.308
1930	WSH	AL	47	188	34	51	11	5	7	38	3	19	19	.271
1930	**SLB**	**AL**	**101**	**396**	**81**	**129**	**25**	**7**	**30**	**100**	**14**	**48**	**35**	**.326**
1931	**SLB**	**AL**	**151**	**591**	**114**	**194**	**42**	**10**	**24**	**105**	**9**	**80**	**41**	**.328**
1932	**SLB**	**AL**	**150**	**572**	**88**	**171**	**28**	**9**	**17**	**104**	**12**	**92**	**35**	**.299**
1933	WSH	AL	132	549	97	163	35	10	10	64	5	42	32	.297
1934	DET	AL	151	614	106	187	38	7	13	100	5	65	38	.305
1935	DET	AL	147	590	87	172	34	6	9	111	5	56	31	.292
1936	DET	AL	147	572	122	180	33	8	24	125	14	85	50	.315
1937	DET	AL	79	181	30	43	11	1	4	35	0	35	18	.238
1938	WSH	AL	38	57	6	9	3	0	2	8	0	8	5	.158
Career Totals			**2287**	**8656**	**1482**	**2735**	**500**	**173**	**248**	**1612**	**176**	**949**	**585**	**.316**
SLB (3 Yrs)		**AL**	**402**	**1559**	**283**	**494**	**95**	**26**	**71**	**309**	**35**	**220**	**111**	**.317**

Satchel Paige

Leroy "Satchel" Paige began playing baseball in the 1920s after being expelled from reform school. His time in professional baseball started with the Negro Leagues' Birmingham Black Barons in 1927 and ended in 1965 pitching for the Kansas City Athletics. In between he became the biggest draw in Negro League history and the biggest showman within the game itself. He spent two and a half seasons with the St. Louis Browns and was twice selected to represent the team and the A.L. in the All-Star Game (1952 and 1953).

Satchel was a six-time All-Star in the Negro Leagues playing for the Pittsburgh Crawfords and the Kansas City Monarchs during the 1930s and 1940s before being signed at age 42 by Bill Veeck to play for the Cleveland Indians in their World Championship season of 1948. Veeck had signed Larry Doby to join the Indians in July 1947 as the second African American to break the color barrier shortly after Jackie Robinson's debut that year. Satchel would become the seventh Black player in the majors when he joined the Indians. He played for Cleveland the following season but was released when Veeck had to sell the team as part of a divorce settlement. Satchel would join Veeck once more when Veeck bought the St. Louis Browns in July of 1951. When Veeck was forced to sell the team in 1953, Paige was out of professional baseball. He continued barnstorming across the nation for the next decade until Kansas City Athletics owner Charlie Finley coaxed him into pitching one more game in the big leagues in September 1965. Back on a big-league mound, Satchel pitched three innings of one-hit shutout ball to add to the myth and legend of the player named Satchel Paige.

Inducted into the Hall of Fame as a player in 1971 by the Negro League Committee

Position: *Pitcher*

Batted: *Right* **Threw:** *Right*

Height: *6' 3"* **Weight:** *180 lbs.*

Born: *July 7, 1906, in Mobile, AL*

Died: *June 8, 1982, in Kansas City, MO*

Buried: *Forest Hill Cemetery, Kansas City, MO*

Debut (Negro League): *1927, with the Birmingham Black Barons*

Debut (MLB): *July 9, 1948, with the Cleveland Indians*

Final game: *September 25, 1965, with the Kansas City Athletics*

Postseason: *Negro League World Series Champion (1942), MLB World Series Champion (1948), A.L. Pennant (1948)*

Awards & Recognition: *6× Negro League All-Star (1933, 1934, 1936, 1941–1943), 2× MLB All-Star (1952, 1953),*

Numbers worn in St. Louis: *Browns (22, 29)*

Satchel Paige – HOF Career Playing Stats – WAR: 46.9

YEAR(S)	SEASONS	TEAM	LEAGUE	W	L	ERA	G	CG	SHO	SV	IP	H	HR	BB	SO
1927 - 1930	4	BBB	NNL	36	17	2.93	86	36	6	8	491	432	2	104	472
1931	1	CCU	NNL	1	1	2.13	5	2	1	0	25.1	19	2	4	180
1933 - 1934, 1936	3	PC	NNL2	25	10	2.16	42	30	7	2	296	213	9	74	301
1940 - 1947	8	KCM	NAL	32	23	2.36	89	20	4	1	449.1	368	2	99	407
1941	1	NBY	NNL2	1	0	2.00	1	1	0	0	9	5	0	0	8
1943	1	MRS	NAL	1	0	0.00	1	0	0	0	5	0	0	2	7
1948 - 1949	2	CLE	AL	10	8	2.78	52	4	2	6	155.2	131	6	55	97
1951 - 1953	**3**	**SLB**	**AL**	**18**	**23**	**3.57**	**126**	**3**	**2**	**27**	**317.1**	**297**	**23**	**125**	**190**
1965	1	KCA	AL	0	0	0.00	1	0	0	0	3	1	0	0	1
Career Totals	**22**			**124**	**82**	**2.73**	**403**	**96**	**22**	**44**	**1751.2**	**1466**	**44**	**463**	**1501**

Getty Images

Rick Ferrell

Rick Ferrell began his Hall of Fame career with the St. Louis Browns in 1929 and played with the team through 1933 and again from 1941 to 1943, just missing their pennant-winning season of 1944. He was regarded as one of the best catchers in baseball in the 1930s and early 1940s. In fact, Ferrell had caught more games than any other American Leaguer (1,806) until Carlton Fisk surpassed him in 1988. Ferrell played for two other teams during his 18-year career. One of the other teams was the Red Sox, where he teamed up with his brother, pitcher Wes Ferrell. The brothers were both selected to play for the A.L. squad in baseball's first All-Star Game in 1933. Ferrell caught all nine innings of that first Midseason Classic and would go on to be an All-Star seven more times.

Ferrell made it to the Browns by declaring for free agency after the 1928 season, long before it became an approved part of the game in 1974. After three years in the minors, Ferrell appealed to Commissioner Kennesaw Mountain Landis that ownership was colluding to keep him in the Minors. After reviewing Ferrell's evidence, the Commissioner concurred and granted Ferrell permission to sign as a free agent with the major league team of his choice. He chose the Browns and debuted with the team as a 23-year-old. He spent eight seasons as a Brown and wound up hitting .270, lower than his career average of .281. His career home run total was only 28 dingers, but he was there every day handling pitchers behind the plate. He may have had the most unenviable situation when he played for the Washington Senators, whose pitching rotation consisted of four knuckleball pitchers. Defensively, Ferrell handled them just fine, as he did all pitchers throughout his career.

Inducted into the Hall of Fame as a player in 1984 by the Veterans Committee

Position: *Catcher*

Batted: *Right* **Threw:** *Right*

Height: *5' 10"* **Weight:** *160 lbs.*

Born: *October 12, 1905, in Durham, NC*

Died: *July 27, 1995, in Bloomfield Hills, MI*

Buried: *New Garden Cemetery, Greensboro, NC*

Debut: *April 19, 1929, with the St. Louis Browns*

Final game: *September 14, 1947, with the Washington Senators*

Postseason: *N/A*

Awards & Recognition: *8× All-Star (1933–1938, 1944, 1945)*

Number worn in St. Louis: *Browns (8)*

Rick Ferrell – HOF Playing Career – WAR: 30.8, Slash Line: .281 / .378 / .363

SEASON	TEAM	LG	G	AB	R	H	2B	3B	HR	RBI	SB	BB	SO	BA
1929	**SLB**	**AL**	**64**	**144**	**21**	**33**	**6**	**1**	**0**	**20**	**1**	**32**	**10**	**.229**
1930	**SLB**	**AL**	**101**	**314**	**43**	**84**	**18**	**4**	**1**	**41**	**1**	**46**	**10**	**.268**
1931	**SLB**	**AL**	**117**	**386**	**47**	**118**	**30**	**4**	**3**	**57**	**2**	**56**	**12**	**.306**
1932	**SLB**	**AL**	**126**	**438**	**67**	**138**	**30**	**5**	**2**	**65**	**5**	**66**	**18**	**.315**
1933	**SLB**	**AL**	**22**	**72**	**8**	**18**	**2**	**0**	**1**	**5**	**2**	**12**	**4**	**.250**
1933	BOS	AL	118	421	50	125	19	4	3	72	2	58	19	.297
1934	BOS	AL	132	437	50	130	29	4	1	48	0	66	20	.297
1935	BOS	AL	133	458	54	138	34	4	3	61	5	65	15	.301
1936	BOS	AL	121	410	59	128	27	5	8	55	0	65	17	.312
1937	BOS	AL	18	65	8	20	2	0	1	4	0	15	4	.308
1937	WSH	AL	86	279	31	64	6	0	1	32	1	50	18	.229
1938	WSH	AL	135	411	55	120	24	5	1	58	1	75	17	.292
1939	WSH	AL	87	274	32	77	13	1	0	31	1	41	12	.281
1940	WSH	AL	103	326	35	89	18	2	0	28	1	47	15	.273
1941	WSH	AL	21	66	8	18	5	0	0	13	1	15	4	.273
1941	**SLB**	**AL**	**100**	**321**	**30**	**81**	**14**	**3**	**2**	**23**	**2**	**52**	**22**	**.252**
1942	**SLB**	**AL**	**99**	**273**	**20**	**61**	**6**	**1**	**0**	**26**	**0**	**33**	**13**	**.223**
1943	**SLB**	**AL**	**74**	**209**	**12**	**50**	**7**	**0**	**0**	**20**	**0**	**34**	**14**	**.239**
1944	WSH	AL	99	339	14	94	11	1	0	25	2	46	13	.277
1945	WSH	AL	91	286	33	76	12	1	1	38	2	43	13	.266
1947	WSH	AL	37	99	10	30	11	0	0	12	0	14	7	.303
Career Totals			**1884**	**6028**	**687**	**1692**	**324**	**45**	**28**	**734**	**29**	**931**	**277**	**.281**
SLB (8 Yrs)		**AL**	**703**	**2157**	**248**	**583**	**113**	**18**	**9**	**257**	**13**	**331**	**103**	**.270**

Getty Images

Bill Veeck

Bill Veeck was a baseball man and master entertainer. He inherited his love of the game from his father, who was president of the Chicago Cubs. He became a maverick entertainer, always looking for ways to attract people to games and have fun. Veeck's resume is an endless list of gimmicks and fan opportunities. He brought fireworks into the stadiums, sent "little people" to the plate, and found managers in the grandstands. He even started a riot by blowing up disco records on the field.

More importantly, he was an advocate for equality in baseball. As owner of the Cleveland Indians, he signed Larry Doby as the A.L.'s first Black player (second in the majors after Jackie Robinson). He then added Satchel Paige to help the team win a World Series in 1948. Forced to sell the Indians the following year as part of his divorce settlement, Veeck saw a perfect storm forming in St. Louis in 1951. The Browns and Sportsman's Park were for sale, and their tenant Cardinals were facing issues as well. Cardinals owner Fred Saigh was in trouble with the IRS and headed to jail. Veeck's plan was to buy the Browns and run the Cardinals out of town.

It seemed like a plan that could work—almost. Veeck owned the stadium and could terminate the Cardinals' lease. In the meantime, Veeck set about winning over St. Louis fans. He sponsored jazz bands, Bat Days, circuses, and even the Harlem Globetrotters playing on a court laid out at second base. Then brewery owner August Busch bought the Cardinals and the stadium, and Veeck knew he could not compete. He sold out but would make a comeback in Chicago and would even win another pennant there in 1959. What would St. Louis baseball be like today if Veeck had run the Cardinals out of town?

Getty Images

Inducted into the Hall of Fame as a pioneer/executive in 1991 by the Veterans Committee

Teams Owned: *Cleveland Indians (1946–1949), St. Louis Browns (1951–1953), Chicago White Sox (1958–1961, 1975–1981)*

Born: *February 9, 1914, in Chicago, IL*

Died: *January 2, 1986, in Chicago, IL*

Buried: *Cremated; ashes scattered in Lake Michigan*

Postseason: *World Series Champion (1948), 2x A.L. Pennant (1948, 1959)*

Bill Veeck – HOF Career Owner / Executive Stats

YEAR(S)	SEASONS	TEAM	LEAGUE	WON	LOST	W-L%	TIES	GAMES	PENNANTS	CHAMPIONSHIPS
1946 - 1949	4	CLE	AL	334	283	.536	6	623	1	1
1951 - 1953	**3**	**SLB**	**AL**	**170**	**292**	**.367**	**1**	**463**	**0**	**0**
1959 - 1961	3	CHW	AL	267	203	.564	3	473	1	0
1975 - 1981	7	CHW	AL	497	574	.463	2	1073	0	0
Career Totals	**17**			**1268**	**1352**	**.482**	**12**	**2632**	**2**	**1**

Getty Images

Willard Brown

Negro League icon Buck O'Neil called Willard Brown "the most natural player I ever saw." When Brown and Hank Thompson took the field together on July 20, 1947, the St. Louis Browns became Major League Baseball's first team to field two African Americans after Jackie Robinson broke the color barrier in April 1947. While Thompson had been the third Black player to cross the white chalk lines days earlier, Brown became the fourth. Today that historic moment is forgotten just like the second crew to land on the moon decades later.

This progressive move by the Browns was made in Major League Baseball's southernmost city. Their city-mate Cardinals would not integrate for another seven years. But the Browns were hoping these two players from the Kansas City Monarchs could help them win. Brown had led the Monarchs to six pennants from 1937 to 1946, and legendary great Josh Gibson nicknamed him "Home Run Brown" for his prodigious blasts. Brown became the first Black player to hit a home run in A.L. history, an inside-the-park shot against the Detroit Tigers and future Hall of Fame pitcher Hal Newhouser. Brown, however, became frustrated with the Browns' losing ways and the racist taunts from St. Louis fans. He hit only .179 in 21 games before being released in late August. Whether he was let go due to his play or a contract clause that required the Browns to pay additional money to the Monarchs if the duo stayed until the end of the season continues to be a matter subject to speculation. Brown went to Puerto Rico that winter and had the first of two Triple Crown seasons batting .432 with 27 home runs and 86 RBIs in 60 games to earn a new moniker, "Ese Hombre" or "That Man."

St. Louis Browns Historical Society

Inducted into the Hall of Fame as a player in 2006 by the Negro League Committee

Positions: *Outfield, Shortstop*

Batted: *Right* **Threw:** *Right*

Height: *5' 11"* **Weight:** *200 lbs.*

Born: *June 26, 1916, in Shreveport, LA*

Died: *August 4, 1996, in Houston, TX*

Buried: *Houston National Cemetery, Houston, TX*

Debut (Negro League): *1936, with the Kansas City Monarchs*

Debut (MLB): *July 19, 1947, with the St. Louis Browns*

Final game: *MLB: August 17, 1947, with the St. Louis Browns, Negro Leagues 1951 with the Kansas City Monarchs*

Postseason: *Negro League World Series Champion (1942), 6× Negro A.L. Pennant (1937, 1939–1942, 1946)*

Awards & Recognition: *7× Negro League All-Star (1936–1937, 1942, 1942 (2nd), 1943, 1948, 1948 (2nd)), Negro A.L. Batting Leader (1947)*

Nicknames: *Ese Hombre, Home Run*

Number worn in St. Louis: *Browns (15)*

Willard Brown– Career HOF Stats – WAR: 20.2, Slash Line: .351 / .398 / .579

SEASON	TEAM	LG	G	AB	R	H	2B	3B	HR	RBI	SB	BB	SO	BA
1937	KCM	NAL	56	214	51	81	11	10	10	60	10	19		.379
1938	KCM	NAL	47	180	34	62	16	4	7	48	20	11		.344
1939	KCM	NAL	44	174	37	64	15	7	3	42	8	9		.368
1940	KCM	NAL	2	7	0	0	0	0	0	0	0	0		.000
1941	KCM	NAL	38	144	31	49	7	4	6	32	10	16		.340
1942	KCM	NAL	35	142	25	48	6	2	4	26	2	8		.338
1943	KCM	NAL	53	197	33	67	13	2	7	31	4	16		.340
1944	KCM	NAL	3	9	2	3	0	0	0	1	1	1		.333
1945	Did not play – Military Service													
1946	KCM	NAL	38	145	30	48	11	6	3	27	3	7		.331
1947	**SLB**	**AL**	**21**	**67**	**4**	**12**	**3**	**0**	**1**	**6**	**2**	**0**	**7**	**.179**
1947	KCM	NAL	48	199	42	75	22	7	6	64	12	16		.377
1948	KCM	NAL	46	174	43	71	23	2	7	54	8	22		.408
Career Totals			**431**	**1652**	**332**	**580**	**127**	**44**	**54**	**391**	**80**	**125**	**7**	**.351**
SLB (1 Yr)		**AL**	**21**	**67**	**4**	**12**	**3**	**0**	**1**	**6**	**2**	**0**	**7**	**.179**

Getty Images

1916 St. Louis Giants
Missouri Historical Society, St. Louis

1928 St. Louis Stars
Missouri Historical Society, St. Louis

Stars Park, located at the corner of Market Street and Compton Avenue
Missouri Historical Society, St. Louis

Players from the Negro Leagues

Ever since Alexander Cartwright (not Abner Doubleday) drafted a set of rules in 1845 that became the foundation for today's game, Black and White players have played and enjoyed the game of baseball. It was becoming the nation's pastime for all Americans. Unfortunately, for nearly a century Black and White players did not play against each other. Paralleling a segregated American society, the game of baseball remained two separated institutions until April 15, 1947, when Jackie Robinson broke through baseball's color barrier in his first game with the Brooklyn Dodgers. Up until that point, African American ballplayers had played within the confines of their own leagues. There would often be barnstorming games played between members of the different leagues, but even those were frowned upon by some.

The following pages highlight those members of the National Baseball Hall of Fame who played in those segregated Negro Leagues on teams from St. Louis, including the St. Louis Giants (1906–1920) and the St. Louis Stars (1921–1931). The Giants had begun playing in independent leagues before becoming an inaugural member of the newly formed Negro National League (NNL) in 1920. The following season, new ownership took over the team and changed its name to the Stars. The Stars went on to be one of the best teams in the league's history. They won three championships before the league's demise after the 1931 season. It was through the play of these two teams and their players that the rich and winning baseball history of the Negro Leagues in St. Louis was written. Three Hall of Fame inductees (Willard Brown, Minnie Miñoso, and Satchel Paige) were former Negro League players who made it to the big leagues once Jackie Robinson opened the door. While their stories are included within the sections of their major league teams, they must be remembered alongside the following Negro League Hall of Famers who played before that door opened. Had these men been able to cross Major League Baseball's white chalk lines, they too would have starred in the big leagues. While history did not allow that to happen, their time and contributions have earned them a special place in St. Louis baseball history.

Several of the players described here spent many years playing with other teams in the many different leagues that comprise the history of the Negro Leagues. Negro League history is dotted with teams and leagues that rose and failed after the first iteration of the Negro National League in 1920. As Negro League baseball tried survive the financial burdens of the Great Depression, leagues like the Eastern Colored League (ECL - 1923), the American Negro League (ANL - 1929), Negro Southern League (NSL - 1932), and the Negro American League (NAL - 1932) were formed and perpetuated the strong tradition of African American baseball. Within these leagues were the historic names of great Negro League teams like the Birmingham Black Barons (BBB), Chicago American Giants (CAG), Homestead Grays (HG), Indianapolis ABCs (ABC), Kansas City Monarchs (KCM), Newark Eagles (NE), and Pittsburgh Crawfords (PC). Despite the leagues' ongoing struggles, Negro League baseball offered an aggressive and exciting style of play that quenched the thirst of African Americans living within a segregated world.

James "Cool Papa" Bell

James "Cool Papa" Bell played in the Negro Leagues from 1922 through 1946. As a lifelong resident of St. Louis, Bell is probably the most heralded of the St. Louis Negro League ball players due to his time spent with the St. Louis Stars. Bell was an eight-time Negro League All-Star with a lifetime batting average of .325. His skills and career are aptly summarized on his Hall of Fame plaque, which reads: "Combined speed, daring and batting skill to rank among best players in Negro Leagues. Contemporaries rated him the fastest man on base paths. Hit over .300 regularly. Topping .400 on occasion. Played 29 summers and 21 winters of professional baseball".

Bell came into the game as a 19-year-old left-handed pitcher, but his talent soon dictated that he should be an everyday centerfielder. Once he was put in the field, his skills became legendary. The fabled Satchel Paige provided the best description of Bell's speed when he said: "Let me tell you about Cool Papa Bell. One time he hit a line drive right past my ear. I turned around and saw the ball hit his rear end as he slid into second." Paige adds that Bell "was so fast he could flip the light switch and be in bed before the room got dark."

Bell was the epitome of the early Negro League player, showcasing an aggressive, daring, and exciting style of play that became so popular that their teams would often outdraw the major league teams of their shared cities. While his Stars teams won Negro League pennants (1928, 1930, and 1931), he was also part of two other fabled teams from the different leagues that played under the Negro League banner. After the Stars and the league folded following the 1931 season due to the financial constraints of the Great Depression, Bell played for the Homestead Grays and the Pittsburgh Crawfords teams that featured six other future Hall of Famers: Oscar Charleston, Josh Gibson, Judy Johnson, Biz Mackey, Satchel Paige, and Jud Wilson. To honor the St. Louis Negro League star and the history of the Negro Leagues in St. Louis, the St. Louis Cardinals have erected a bronze statue of Bell within their ring of Cardinal Hall of Famers' statues outside Busch Stadium III.

Getty Images

Inducted into the Hall of Fame as a player in 1974 by the Negro League Committee

Positions: *Center Field, Pitcher*

Batted: *Both* **Threw:** *Left*

Height: *6' 0"* **Weight:** *155 lbs.*

Born: *May 17, 1903, in Starkville, MS*

Died: *March 7, 1991, in St. Louis, MO*

Buried: *St. Peter's Cemetery, St. Louis, MO*

Debut: *1922, with the St. Louis Stars*

Final game: *1946, with the Homestead Grays*

Postseason: *3× Negro National League Champions (1928, 1930, 1931*), NNL Pennant (1925**), 3× NNL2 World Series Champion (1935, 1943, 1944), 1x NNL2 Pennant (1945).*

Awards & Recognition: *8× All-Star (1933–1936, 1942, 1942 (2nd), 1943, 1944)*

Nickname: *Cool Papa*

**The Stars finished in first place in league play, but there were no post-season games played. **The Stars came in second, losing a Championship Series to the Kansas City Monarchs.*

James "Cool Papa" Bell – HOF Career Playing Stats – WAR: 34.7, Slash Line: .325 / .394 / .446

YEAR(S)	SEASONS	TEAM	LEAGUE	G	AB	R	H	2B	3B	HR	RBI	SB	BB	SO	BA
1922 - 1931	**10**	**SLS**	**NNL**	**691**	**2761**	**699**	**899**	**176**	**41**	**47**	**364**	**195**	**275**	**NA**	**.326**
1929, 1942	2	CAG	NN2, NAL	30	115	17	32	4	2	0	8	0	13	NA	.278
1932	1	DW	EWL	29	119	28	38	6	2	0	13	8	11	NA	.319
1933 - 1937	5	PC	NN2	240	965	230	307	42	15	8	113	49	113	NA	.318
1938 - 1941	Played in Mexico														
1932, 1943 - 1946	5	HG	EWL, NN2	212	807	178	272	34	12	2	98	33	119	NA	.337
Career Totals	**21**			**1202**	**4767**	**1152**	**1548**	**262**	**72**	**57**	**596.0**	**285**	**531**	**NA**	**.325**

Getty Images

Oscar Charleston

It has never been debated whether Oscar Charleston was one of the best players in the Negro Leagues. His stats seal that deal and tell a tale of one of the best in the game's history. Negro League veteran and goodwill ambassador Buck O'Neil described Charleston as "a tremendous left-handed hitter who could also bunt, steal a hundred bases a year, and cover center field as well as anyone before him or since. . . . He was like Ty Cobb, Babe Ruth and Tris Speaker rolled into one." While hitting for average like Cobb, Charleston had more home run power than Cobb. Defensively he was the equal of the great centerfielder Tris Speaker. His play today would be compared to that of Willie Mays.

Major League Baseball's recent statistical review and inclusion of the Negro Leagues into their record books lifted Charleston into the third spot in all-time career batting average (.365*), trailing only baseball's newly crowned champion Josh Gibson (.372) and Ty Cobb (.367). Charleston's three Triple Crowns remain the most of any player in the game. The first of those three Triple Crowns came during Charleston's second professional season, his lone season (1921) in St. Louis with the Giants. That season turned out to be the best year of his career. That year Charleston hit .433 for the Giants and led the league in home runs, runs, and RBIs. When the Giants were having financial issues and in transition to new ownership in 1922, Charleston chose to return to his former team, the Indianapolis ABCs. In 1976 he was inducted into Baseball's Hall of Fame with a plaque highlighting a career in which he was "rated among all-time greats of Negro Leagues. Versatile star batted well over .300 most years. Speed, strong arm and fielding instincts made him standout center fielder. Later moved to first base. Also managed several teams during forty years in Negro Baseball." Hall of Fame manager John McGraw best summarized Charleston's abilities by saying, "If Oscar Charleston isn't the greatest baseball player in the world, then I'm no judge of baseball talent."

Getty Images

Inducted into the Hall of Fame as a player in 1976 by the Negro League Committee

Positions: *Center Field, First Base, Manager*

Batted: *Left* **Threw:** *Left*

Height: *5' 8"* **Weight:** *185 lbs.*

Born: *October 14, 1896, in Indianapolis, IN*

Died: *October 5, 1954, in Philadelphia, PA*

Buried: *Floral Park Cemetery, Indianapolis, IN*

Debut: *1915, with the Indianapolis ABCs*

Final game: *1941, with the Philadelphia Stars*

Postseason: *Negro League Championship (1935), 2× Negro National League Pennant (1933, 1936)*

Awards & Recognition: *Negro National League Batting Leader (1921), 2× Eastern Colored League Batting Leader (1924, 1925), 3× Triple Crown (1921, 1924, 1925), 3× East–West All -Star Game (1933–1935)*

**Since the reconciliation of the Negro Leagues and major league records has taken place, some entities like Major League Baseball have shown Charleston's career batting mark at .363. This reconciliation can vary dependent upon the scope of the leagues, teams, and scheduling data used. The National Baseball Hall of Fame and Baseball-reference define Charleston's career batting mark at .365.*

Oscar Charleston – Career Managerial Stats

YEAR(S)	SEASONS	TEAM	LEAGUE	WON	LOST	W-L%	TIES	GAMES	EJECTIONS	PENNANTS	CHAMPIONSHIPS
1924 - 1926	3	HBG	ECL	105	77	.577	1	183	NA	0	0
1929	1	HIL	ANL	0	4	.000	0	4	NA	0	0
1933 - 1940	9	TC	NN2	269	224	.546	14	507	NA	3	0
1941, 1948	2	PS	NN2	46	72	.390	8	126	NA	0	0
Career Totals	**14**			**420**	**377**	**.527**	**23**	**820**	**NA**	**3**	**0**

Oscar Charleston – HOF Career Playing Stats – WAR: 48.1, Slash Line: .365 / .449 / .615

YEAR(S)	SEASONS	TEAM	LEAGUE	G	AB	R	H	2B	3B	HR	RBI	SB	BB	SO	BA
1920, 1922 - 1923	3	ABC	NNL	277	1055	253	384	70	35	35	255	66	126	NA	.364
1921	**1**	**SLG**	**NNL**	**77**	**284**	**104**	**123**	**17**	**12**	**15**	**91**	**32**	**41**	**NA**	**.433**
1924 - 1927	4	HBG	ECL	242	877	271	343	77	16	58	277	82	162	NA	.391
1929	1	HIL	ANL	78	278	69	100	23	7	7	62	8	54	NA	.360
1929	1	HG	ANL	4	13	2	6	2	0	0	2	0	2	NA	.462
1933 - 1937, 1939 - 1940	7	PC / TC	NN2 / NAL	237	801	154	251	52	10	29	167	21	90	NA	.313
1941	1	PS	NN2	2	4	0	2	0	0	0	1	1	2	NA	.500
Career Totals	**17**			**917**	**3312**	**853**	**1209**	**241**	**80**	**144**	**855.0**	**210**	**477**	**NA**	**.365**

Getty Images

Willie Wells

From Bobby Wallace to Marty Marion to Ozzie Smith, St. Louis's baseball history includes many of the greatest players ever to play shortstop. That list also includes the Negro League great Willie Wells. Cool Papa Bell opined: "The shortstops I've seen, Wells could cover ground better than any of them. Willie Wells was the greatest shortstop in the world." With little debate, the legendary Negro League owner Effa Manley called him "The finest shortstop, black or white."

Willie Wells played in the Negro Leagues between 1924 and 1948. Hitting .330 over his career, Wells joined the St. Louis Stars in 1924 and stayed with the team until it folded along with the rest of the league in 1931. He led the Leage in home runs three times while in St. Louis and won the Triple Crown in 1930. His Cooperstown plaque describes Wells as a player who "combined superior batting skills, slick fielding, and speed on the bases to become a 10-time All Star in the Negro Leagues. A power-hitting shortstop with great hands. Ranks among the all-time Negro League leaders in doubles, triples, home runs and stolen bases. Played on three pennant-winning teams with the St. Louis Stars. One with the Chicago American Giants and one with the Newark Eagles. Overall, he played for many Negro League clubs with stints in the Canadian, Mexican and Cuban Leagues. Player-manager in the Negro Leagues as well." Wells was part of the Newark Eagles famed "million-dollar infield" in the late 1930s alongside future Hall of Famers Mule Suttles and Ray Dandridge. Wells succinctly summarized his view of life and baseball: "I didn't want to do anything but play baseball. That was my life, and it was good to me. Baseball is still nothing but hit the ball and catch the ball."

Missouri Historical Society, St. Louis

Inducted into the Hall of Fame as a player in 1997 by the Veterans Committee

Positions: *Shortstop, Third Base*

Batted: *Right* **Threw:** *Right*

Height: *5' 9"* **Weight:** *170 lbs.*

Born: *October 23, 1922, in Austin, TX*

Died: *January 4, 1994, in Austin, TX*

Buried: *Texas State Cemetery, Austin, TX*

Debut: *1944, with the Chicago American Giants*

Final game: *1948, with the Memphis Red Sox*

Postseason: *3× Negro National League Champions (1928, 1930, 1931*), NNL Pennant (1925**), 2× NN2 Pennant (1934, 1939)*

Awards & Recognition: *10× Negro League All-Star (1933–1935, 1937–1938, 1939, 1939 (2nd), 1942, 1942 (2nd), 1945), National Negro League Batting Leader (1930), Triple Crown (1930)*

Nickname: *The Devil*

**The Stars finished in first place in league play, but there were no post-season games played. **The Stars came in second, losing a Championship Series to the Kansas City Monarchs.*

Willie Wells – Career Managerial Stats

YEAR(S)	SEASONS	TEAM	LEAGUE	WON	LOST	W-L%	TIES	GAMES	EJECTIONS	PENNANTS	CHAMPIONSHIPS
1942, 1945	2	NE	NN2	47	43	.522	3	93	NA	0	0
1945	1	NBY	NN2	3	7	.300	0	10	NA	0	0
1947	1	IC	NAL	14	29	.326	0	43	NA	0	0
Career Totals	**3**			**64**	**79**	**.448**	**3**	**146**	**NA**	**0**	**0**

Willie Wells – HOF Career Playing Stats – WAR: 49.5, Slash Line: .330 / .407 / .535

YEAR(S)	SEASONS	TEAM	LEAGUE	G	AB	R	H	2B	3B	HR	RBI	SB	BB	SO	BA
1924 - 1931	**8**	**SLS**	**NNL**	**609**	**2627**	**2282**	**602**	**803**	**160**	**36**	**119**	**608**	**115**	**325**	**.352**
1929, 1933 - 1935	4	CAG	NNL	125	563	499	110	144	30	13	5	76	27	49	.289
1932	1	DW	EWL	29	125	113	20	32	13	2	0	20	3	9	.283
1932, 1937	2	HG	EWL / NN2	14	61	55	9	11	1	1	2	9	0	4	.200
1936 - 1939, 1942, 1945	6	NE	NN2	170	723	637	154	200	32	8	13	108	11	70	.314
1945 - 1946	2	NBY	NN2	27	114	101	10	29	6	0	0	10	2	9	.287
1946	1	BEG	NN2	53	218	197	19	59	13	3	1	36	1	18	.299
1947	1	IC	NAL	6	21	19	2	6	0	1	0	3	0	1	.316
1948	1	MRS	NAL	6	19	17	6	8	2	1	0	3	1	2	.471
Career Totals	**21**			**1039**	**4471**	**3920**	**932**	**1292**	**257**	**65**	**140.0**	**873**	**160**	**487**	**.330**

Missouri Historical Society, St. Louis

James “Biz” Mackey

James Rawley “Biz” Mackey has been heralded as one of the best—if not the best—catcher ever to play in the Negro Leagues. His connection to St. Louis was very brief. It came in 1921 as a member of the St. Louis Giants. After having played the season with the Indianapolis ABCs, Mackey joined the Giants to play in an October 1920 City Series with the Major League Baseball St. Louis Cardinals before rejoining the ABCs the following season. While his career as a player and manager lasted until 1947, his playing days came a generation too early for him to make it into the major leagues..

It was a career in which he was called “the total package,” as shown by Cool Papa Bell’s statement that “Actually, as much as I admired (Roy) Campanella as a catcher all-around, and (Josh) Gibson as a hitter, I believe Biz Mackey was the best catcher I ever saw.” Mackey was unsurpassed behind the plate as a defender and a thrower. His throws to ward off base stealers came with extreme accuracy and velocity from a squatting position. While barely literate, Mackey was one of the most astute students of the game—a trait that would later make him one of the Negro League’s best managers. Mackey’s Cooperstown plaque summarizes his career as “a superb defensive catcher and natural leader who could play all positions. Starred in 1920s with Hilldales of Philadelphia, leading them to 1925 Negro Leagues World Series title. A line drive switch-hitter whose average topped .300 most seasons. Played in five East-West All-Star games. As player-manager of Baltimore Elite Giants, mentored teenage catcher Roy Campanella. Managed five other future Hall of Famers during tenure with Newark, leading Eagles to only championship in 1946.”

Inducted into the Hall of Fame as a player in 2006 by the Negro League Committee

Positions: *Catcher, Shortstop, First Base, Manager*

Batted: *Both* **Threw:** *Right*

Height: *6’ 1”* **Weight:** *235 lbs.*

Born: *July 27, 1897, in Eagle Pass, TX*

Died: *September 22, 1965, in Los Angeles, CA*

Buried: *Evergreen Cemetery, Los Angeles, CA*

Debut: *1918, with the San Antonio Black Aces*

Final game: *1950, with the Newark Eagles*

Postseason: *3× Negro League Champion (Eastern Colored League, 1925; Negro National League 2, 1934, 1946)*

Awards & Recognition: *5× East–West All-Star Game (1922, 1935, 1936, 1938, 1947), Eastern Colored League Batting Leader (1923)*

James “Biz” Mackey – Career Managerial Stats

YEAR(S)	SEASONS	TEAM	LEAGUE	WON	LOST	W-L%	TIES	GAMES	EJECTIONS	PENNANTS	CHAMPIONSHIPS
1937	1	WEG	NN2	24	37	.393	4	65	NA	0	0
1940 - 1941, 1945 - 1947	5	NE	NN2	162	106	.604	5	273	NA	1	1
Career Totals	**6**			**186**	**143**	**.565**	**9**	**338**	**NA**	**1**	**1**

James “Biz” Mackey – HOF Career Playing Stats – WAR: 25.3, Slash Line: .328 / .390 / .470

YEAR(S)	SEASONS	TEAM	LEAGUE	G	AB	R	H	2B	3B	HR	RBI	SB	BB	SO	BA
1920 - 1922	3	ABC	NNL	232	856	140	292	36	31	17	174	11	65		.341
1920	**1**	**SLG**	**NNL**	**2**	**4**	**1**	**2**	**1**	**0**	**0**	**2**	**1**	**1**	**0**	**.500**
1923 - 1927, 1929	6	HIL	ECL	348	1264	250	445	88	19	28	278	46	130	9	.352
1928	1	BBS	ECL	2	6	2	2	1	1	0	2	0	1		.333
1933	1	PC	NN2	1	4	0	2	0	0	0	0	0	1		.500
1934 - 1935	2	PS	NN2	70	212	22	59	15	1	2	32	1	17		.278
1936 - 1939	4	WEG / BEG	NN2	109	375	49	107	17	3	3	63	1	41		.285
1939 - 1941, 1945 - 1947	6	NE	NN2	137	360	34	102	9	2	2	53	1	42		.283
1940	1	NYC	NN2	1	4	0	2	1	0	0	2	0	1		.500
Career Totals	**22**			**900**	**3081**	**497**	**1011**	**167**	**57**	**52**	**604**	**60**	**298**	**9**	**.328**

Frank Duncan (left) and Biz Mackey
Getty Images

George "Mule" Suttles

In a career that began with the Birmingham Black Barons in 1924, George "Mule" Suttles would spend a total of 21 seasons playing in the Negro Leagues, predominantly with the St. Louis Stars and the Newark Eagles. It was a career that would last until 1944, playing out too soon for Suttles to follow Jackie Robinson into the major leagues. Suttles was a celebrated first baseman/outfielder who became one of the league's premier power hitters.

During his six seasons with the Stars, (1926–1931) Suttles twice led the league in home runs and won the league's Triple Crown in 1926 with a .425 batting average. He would best the .400-mark three other times before ending his career with a .339 batting average. Suttles played a key part in the Stars' three pennants and two Negro League Championships. Even though the Stars won the pennant in 1931, there would be no Championship Series that year because the Negro National League disbanded at season's end due to financial constraints arising from the Great Depression. Despite the Stars' demise, Suttles immediately latched on with the rejuvenated Chicago American Giants, where he won another championship in 1933 before settling in with the Newark Eagles.

Paralleling Major League Baseball's first All-Star Game in 1933, the Negro Leagues run of Midseason Classics also began that year, and Suttles left his mark by hitting the first-ever home run in that series. He would also hit a dramatic three-run homer to win the 1935 Negro League All-Star Game. During the seven-year span between 1933 and 1939, Suttles played in five of the Negro Leagues' East–West All-Star Games. He would retire, as noted on his Hall of Fame plaque, "among all-time Negro Leagues leaders in Doubles, Home runs, RBI, Slugging Percentage and total bases."

Getty Images

Inducted into the Hall of Fame as a player in 2006 by the Negro League Committee

Positions: *First Base, Left Field*

Batted: *Right* **Threw:** *Right*

Height: *6' 1"* **Weight:** *200 lbs.*

Born: *March 31, 1901, in Edgewater, AL*

Died: *July 9, 1966, in Newark, NJ*

Buried: *Glendale Cemetery, Bloomfield, NJ*

Debut: *1924, with the Birmingham Black Barons*

Final game: *1944, with the Newark Eagles*

Postseason: *3× Negro National League Championship (1926, 1930, 1931*), 2x NN2 Pennant (1934, 1939)*

Awards & Recognition: *5× Negro League All-Star Games (1933–1935, 1937, 1939), 2× Negro National Leage Battling Leader (1926, 1928), Triple Crown (1926)*

**The Stars finished in first place in league play, but there were no post-season games played.*

George "Mule" Suttles – Career Managerial Stats

YEAR(S)	SEASONS	TEAM	LEAGUE	WON	LOST	W-L%	TIES	GAMES	EJECTIONS	PENNANTS	CHAMPIONSHIPS
1943 - 1944	2	NE	NN2	58	67	.464	0	125	NA	0	0

George "Mule" Suttles – HOF Career Playing Stats – WAR: 36.6, Slash Line: .339 / .410 / .620

YEAR(S)	SEASONS	TEAM	LEAGUE	G	AB	R	H	2B	3B	HR	RBI	SB	BB	SO	BA
1924 - 1925	2	BBB	NNL	147	516	88	167	27	8	13	108	8	45	NA	.324
1926 - 1931	6	SLS	NNL	376	1401	367	531	108	53	100	450	48	159	NA	.379
1929, 1933 - 1935	4	CAG	NNL / NN2	127	459	80	127	23	4	20	103	12	56	NA	.277
1932	1	DW	EWL	27	97	13	28	11	0	1	22	0	15	NA	.289
1932	1	WAP	EWL	28	90	18	30	11	3	3	26	5	15	NA	.333
1936 - 1940, 1942 - 1944	8	NE	NN2	182	586	143	190	31	5	41	160	10	76	NA	.324
1941	1	NBY	NN2	22	71	11	20	2	2	2	14	2	4	NA	.282
Career Totals	21			909	3220	720	1093	213	75	180	883.0	85	370	NA	.339

Getty Images

St. Louisan Yogi Berra welcomes the 1956 St. Louis Stockham Post American Legion National Champions. Berra played on the Stockham team in 1941.

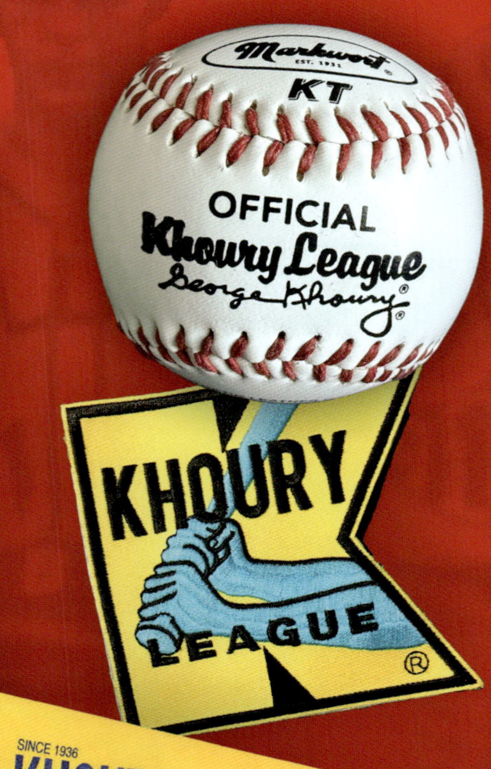

NATIONAL
AMERICAN LEGION
JUNIOR BASEBALL
SECTION "C"
TOURNAMENT

THREE REGIONAL CHAMPIONS

FROM TWELVE STATES

McCORMICK FIELD, NORMAL ILL.
AUGUST 28, 29, & 30, 1950

SPONSORED BY
LOUIS E. DAVIS POST NO. 56
AMERICAN LEGION, BLOOMINGTON, ILL.

JUNIOR BASEBALL COMMISSION

Kaywin Kennedy, *Chairman*

J. W. Scott
Russell Smith
Harry W. Henley
Fred Young
Joe Yuriecі
Deane Miller
George W. Johnston
1950 Commander

Grant W. Coningham
Henry Miller
Arthur P. Kane
Whedon Slater
Ivan Costigan
James Wollrab

James A. Tuley
Adjutant

Ernest Behrmann
Ben Hiltabrand
Morgan Evans
Denzal Burgess
Roy V. Martin
D.M. Jenkins, M.D.
Paul E. McReynolds
1951 Commander

Yogi Berra's 1941 Stockham team photo

Players from St. Louis Who Played Elsewhere

St. Louis has one of the nation's longest and finest traditions of organized baseball, ranging from the little leagues to the major leagues. It's a stellar history, starting with the St. Louis Brown Stockings playing in the N.L.'s inaugural season of 1876. They were followed by the Maroons' entry into the N.L. in 1884, though that franchise soon folded due to the success of the American Association's St. Louis Browns. That success led to the Browns being asked to join the N.L. in 1892, and the team is still flourishing today after having changed their name to the St. Louis Cardinals in 1900. But the foundation of the city's strong baseball history has always been its amateur programs like the Khoury Leagues, formed in St. Louis in 1934 and active across the nation. Many of the men whose plaques hang in the galleries of Cooperstown are alumni of Khoury Legue teams.

Many of St. Louis's American Legion National Championship teams were products of the city's great high school baseball programs. In fact, there was one high school in St. Louis (Beaumont High School) that had more men playing in the major leagues than any other school in the country during a period in the late 1940s and early 1950s. While hundreds of these young players made it to the major leagues after growing up, learning, and playing the game of baseball in St. Louis, three would make it to Cooperstown and be inducted into Baseball's Hall of Fame.

Even though they never played for a team from St. Louis, their stories are included within this anthology as a testament to St. Louis's ties to the amateur level of baseball in America.

Beaumont High School

Yogi Berra

Lawrence "Yogi" Berra was not only one of America's most colorful characters, he was also one of baseball's most honored players and managers. His questionable use of the English language became "Yogi-isms" etched within American culture through media advertisements spread across the nation. His nickname "Yogi" came from his childhood friends, inspired by a character in a matinee movie they had seen together. He grew up playing baseball in St. Louis's Italian neighborhood known as "the Hill" and easily became the best major league player to come out of the St. Louis area. As good as he was, he never played for his hometown Browns or Cardinals—simply because they would not give him a signing bonus like his childhood friend Joe Garagiola received from the Redbirds. The Yankees quickly gave him the $500 bonus he craved, and the rest is history.

The little guy behind the plate became one of the most feared hitters in the game with his quick hands and ability to hit bad pitches out of the park. At the time of his retirement, his 358 home runs were the most hit by a catcher in the history of the game. Although he stood only five-feet seven-inches tall, Yogi (and his accomplishments) stood far above most players. His Hall of Fame catching career consisted of three MVP awards and 18 trips to the All-Star game—including every Midseason Classic between 1948 and 1962. Yogi also made 14 appearances as a player in the World Series (75 games) and became a World Series Champion 10 times—all untouched records in the baseball annals. He would win two additional pennants as a New York manager, one with the A.L. Yankees (1964) and one with the N.L. Mets (1973).

Inducted into the Hall of Fame as a player in 1972 by the BBWAA

Positions: *Catcher, Outfield, Manager*

Batted: *Left* **Threw:** *Right*

Height: *5' 7"* **Weight:** *185 lbs.*

Born: *May 12, 1926, in St. Louis, MO*

Died: *September 22, 2015, in West Caldwell, NJ*

Buried: *Gate of Heaven Catholic Cemetery, East Hanover, NJ*

Debut: *September 22, 1946, with the New York Yankees*

Final game: *May 9, 1965, with the New York Mets*

Postseason: *13× World Series Champion (Player: 1947, 1949–1953, 1956, 1958 1961, 1962; Coach: 1969, 1977, 1978), 5× A.L. Pennant (Player: 1955, 1957, 1960, 1963; Manager: 1964), N.L. Pennant (Manager: 1973)*

Awards & Recognition: *18× All-Star (1948–1958, 1959, 1959 (2nd), 1960, 1960 (2nd), 1961, 1961 (2nd), 1962 (2nd), 3× A.L. MVP (1951, 1954, 1955)*

Yogi Berra – Career Managerial Stats

YEAR(S)	SEASONS	TEAM	LEAGUE	WON	LOST	W-L%	TIES	GAMES	EJECTIONS	PENNANTS	CHAMPIONSHIPS
1964, 1984 - 1985	3	NYY	AL	192	148	.565	2	342	7	1	0
1972 - 1975	4	NYM	NL	292	296	.497	0	588	6	1	0
Career Totals	**7**			**484**	**444**	**.522**	**2**	**930**	**13**	**2**	**0**

Yogi Berra – HOF Career Stats – WAR: 59.5, Slash Line: .285 / .348 / .482

YEAR(S)	SEASONS	TEAM	LEAGUE	G	AB	R	H	2B	3B	HR	RBI	SB	BB	SO	BA
1946 - 1963	18	NYY	AL	2116	7546	1174	2148	321	49	358	1430	26	704	411	.285
1964	1	NYM	NL	4	9	1	2	0	0	0	0	0	0	3	.222
Career Totals	**19**			**2120**	**7555**	**1175**	**2150**	**321**	**49**	**358**	**1430**	**26**	**704**	**414**	**.285**

Getty Images

Earl Weaver

Earl Weaver's big-league story is not as a player but rather as one of the preeminent managers of his era. His career began in St. Louis playing baseball at Beaumont High School—an institution known as the "baseball factory." He had signed with his hometown Cardinals after graduation in 1948 and spent the next several years as a struggling second baseman with little power before getting his first shot managing Knoxville's unaffiliated Class A team in 1956. There he caught the eye of a member of the Baltimore Orioles' farm system, who offered Weaver a job the next season managing at the franchise's lowest level. Weaver put together a string of successful stops within the team's minor league system before being brought up midseason in 1968 as Hank Bauer's replacement to manage a struggling big-league club that had won a pennant two years earlier.

Weaver inherited a well-rounded team of stars led by Frank Robinson's bat and Jim Palmer's pitching. Incorporating the team's other talent, Weaver turned the Orioles into 109-game winners the following year on their way to the World Series against a team that would become known as the "Amazing Mets." The Mets won the Series, but it would be the first of three straight pennants for Weaver's teams. The next year they won the World Series over the Cincinnati Reds before losing to the Pirates in the 1971 Series. In each of those three seasons, the Orioles won at least 100 games.

Weaver was the first manager since the Cardinals' Billy Southworth to claim three straight 100-win seasons. Weaver's teams would total two more consecutive 100-win seasons starting in 1979, a year the Orioles won Weaver's fourth and last pennant. With his retirement after the 1986 season, Weaver's career-winning percentage of .583 ranked sixth among all managers with at least 1,000 wins.

Wikimedia Commons

Inducted into the Hall of Fame as a manager in 1996 by the Veterans Committee

Born: *August 14, 1930, in St. Louis, MO*

Died: *January 19, 2013, aboard Celebrity Silhouette, Caribbean Sea*

Buried: *Cremated*

Managerial Debut: *July 11, 1968, with the Baltimore Orioles*

Last Game Managed: *October 5, 1986, with the Baltimore Orioles*

Postseason: *World Series Champion (1970), 4× A.L. Pennant (1969, 1970, 1971, 1979)*

Awards & Recognition: *4× A.L. All-Star Game Manager (1970–1972, 1980)*

Earl Weaver – HOF Career Managerial Stats

YEAR(S)	TEAM	LEAGUE	WON	LOST	W-L%	TIES	GAMES	EJECTIONS	PENNANTS	CHAMPIONSHIPS
1968	BAL	AL	48	34	.585	0	82	2	0	0
1969	BAL	AL	109	53	.673	0	162	4	1	0
1970	BAL	AL	108	54	.667	0	162	3	1	1
1971	BAL	AL	101	57	.639	0	158	3	1	0
1972	BAL	AL	80	74	.519	0	154	4	0	0
1973	BAL	AL	97	65	.599	0	162	8	0	0
1974	BAL	AL	91	71	.562	0	162	8	0	0
1975	BAL	AL	90	69	.566	0	159	10	0	0
1976	BAL	AL	88	74	.543	0	162	9	0	0
1977	BAL	AL	97	64	.602	0	161	7	0	0
1978	BAL	AL	90	71	.559	0	161	7	0	0
1979	BAL	AL	102	57	.642	0	159	9	1	0
1980	BAL	AL	100	62	.617	0	162	4	0	0
1981	BAL	AL	59	46	.562	0	105	3	0	0
1982	BAL	AL	94	68	.580	1	163	6	0	0
1985	BAL	AL	53	52	.505	0	105	4	0	0
1986	BAL	AL	73	89	.451	0	162	5	0	0
Career Totals			**1480**	**1060**	**.583**	**1**	**2541**	**96**	**4**	**1**

Getty Images

Dick Williams

Like Earl Weaver, Dick Williams grew up in St. Louis attending Beaumont High School before moving to Pasadena, California. Unlike Weaver, Williams made it to the majors in 1951 and stayed for 13 seasons. He hit .260 playing for five different teams as an outfielder and third baseman, and even got to play in the 1953 World Series with the Brooklyn Dodgers.

When Williams's playing days came to an end after the 1964 season, his Hall of Fame managerial career took off. The Red Sox gave him his first opportunity, and he led their AAA team to consecutive championships (1965 and 1966). The next year he was promoted to lead their big-league club. It would be the first of his multiple team turnarounds. In his first year as a big-league manager, he led a Sox team that had finished ninth in the 10-team A.L. in 1966 to within one game of winning the 1967 World Series over the Cardinals.

After the Sox collapsed during the next two seasons Williams was dismissed. He then found another resurrection project with the Oakland Athletics in 1971. A year later his A's were winning the first of two consecutive championships. Falling out of favor with A's owner Charlie Finley, Williams then had stints managing the Angels and Expos before landing in San Diego and leading the Padres to their first World Series appearance in 1984. He would then leave the Padres and manage the Mariners before retiring.

Williams's resume shows a pattern of building up winning teams before heading to the next challenge. He would take his teams to four World Series and two League Championships. Williams joins Bill McKechnie and Bruce Bochy as the only managers to take three franchises to the Series, and he and Lou Pinella remain the only skippers to register seasons of 90 or more wins with four different franchises.

Inducted into the Hall of Fame as a manager in 2008 by the Veterans Committee

Positions: *Outfield, Third Base, First Base, Manager*

Batted: *Right* **Threw:** *Right*

Height: *6' 0"* **Weight:** *190 lbs.*

Born: *May 7, 1929, in St. Louis, MO*

Died: *July 7, 2011, in Las Vegas, NV*

Buried: *Cremated*

Debut: *June 19, 1951, with the Brooklyn Dodgers*

Final game: *September 22, 1964, with the Boston Red Sox*

Postseason: *2× World Series Champion (Manager: 1972, 1973), 2x N.L. Pennant (Player: 1953, Manager: 1984), 1x A.L. Pennant (Manager: 1967)*

Awards & Recognition: *3× A.L. All-Star Game Manager (1968, 1973, 1974), N.L. All-Star Game Manager (1985)*

Dick Williams – HOF Career Managerial Stats

YEAR(S)	SEASONS	TEAM	LEAGUE	WON	LOST	W-L%	TIES	GAMES	EJECTIONS	PENNANTS	CHAMPIONSHIPS
1967 - 1969	3	BOS	AL	260	217	.545	0	477	11	1	0
1971 - 1973	3	OAK	AL	288	190	.603	0	478	11	2	2
1974 - 1976	3	CAL	AL	147	194	.431	0	341	11	0	0
1977 - 1981	5	MON	NL	380	347	.523	0	727	7	0	0
1982 - 1985	4	SDP	NL	337	311	.520	1	649	11	1	0
1986 - 1988	3	SEA	AL	159	192	.453	0	351	6	0	0
Career Totals	**21**			**1571**	**1451**	**.520**	**1**	**3023**	**57**	**4**	**2**

Dick Williams – Career Playing Stats – WAR: 3.4, Slash Line: .260/ .312 / .392

YEAR(S)	SEASONS	TEAM	LG	G	AB	R	H	2B	3B	HR	RBI	SB	BB	SO	BA
1951 - 1956	5	BRO	NL	112	224	27	52	9	2	4	23	0	11	38	.232
1956 - 1958, 1961 - 1962	5	BAL	AL	447	1417	154	361	67	9	25	128	5	115	172	.255
1957	1	CLE	AL	67	205	33	58	7	0	6	17	3	12	19	.283
1959 - 1960	2	KCA	AL	257	908	119	251	64	1	28	140	4	67	128	.276
1963 - 1964	2	BOS	AL	140	205	25	46	10	0	7	23	0	22	35	.224
Career Totals	**13**			**1023**	**2959**	**358**	**768**	**157**	**12**	**70**	**331**	**12**	**227**	**392**	**.260**

Getty Images

NBC broadcasters Tony Kubek (left) and Joe Garagiola (right) before a Major League Baseball game
Getty Images

Sports broadcasters Jack Buck (right) for the St. Louis Cardinals interviews sportswriter Bob Broeg during a game.
Getty Images

Ford C. Frick
Wikimedia Commons

Ford C. Frick Award Winners—Broadcasters

The Ford C. Frick Award was created in 1978 and is named after a former Commissioner of Major League Baseball. It is presented annually by the National Baseball Hall of Fame to a broadcaster for "major contributions to baseball." Though they are sometimes erroneously referred to as "Hall of Famers," honorees are not inducted into the Hall of Fame. Their plaques and memories reside in a separate wing of the Cooperstown institution.

The criteria for selection are a "commitment to excellence, quality of broadcasting abilities, reverence within the game, popularity with fans, and recognition by peers." To be considered for the award, an active or retired broadcaster must have a minimum of 10 years of continuous major league broadcast service with a ball club, network, or a combination of the two.

Radio coverage of baseball first came to St. Louis on KMOX radio in 1926, five years after the first radio broadcast of a 1921 game between the Phillies and the Pirates. St. Louis's reputation as a sports leader is directly attributable to its supportive and knowledgeable fan base. Their love and knowledge of the game has been nurtured for decades and encouraged by broadcasters with a special talent for bringing the game to the people. In the days before television, when there was only radio, the announcers painted a picture of the game for the fans with their words and delivery. They taught fans the nuances of the game and kept them on the edge of their seats waiting for the next pitch. In the decades since those first radio broadcasts, St. Louis has been blessed with many of the best broadcasters ever to cover baseball. Five of these men who were behind the microphone in St. Louis have been recognized in Cooperstown as recipients of broadcasting's Ford Frick Award for their contributions to the game.

Jack Buck

Jack Buck's voice became the soundtrack of summer for generations of St. Louis fans from their childhood through retirement. It was a voice that echoed across porches and through windows of neighborhoods, painting pictures of Cardinals games being played out within the minds of those listening to their radios. His commentary rang out not only across the St. Louis region but also across much of the nation due to the strong 50,000-watt signal of Cardinal radio partner KMOX and Buck's many broadcasts on multiple national affiliate networks over the years.

Buck began his career calling games for the minor league affiliates of the St. Louis Cardinals after his graduation from Ohio State University. He would make it to the big-league team's broadcast booth in 1954, sharing play-by-play coverage with fellow Ford Frick winner Harry Caray until the latter's departure in 1970. During his tenure with the Cardinals Buck shared the microphone with many of baseball's most memorable voices, including Milo Hamilton, Joe Garagiola, Mike Shannon, and even his son Joe Buck. But it was always the special calm of Buck's raspy voice, speaking with a touch of irony, that made his play-by-play so unique. What made Buck a "winner" in the booth was the simple fact that he was as much a fan of the game as were his listeners. And he left us with many of the most memorable calls of our generation.

A very brief summary of Buck's greatest hits (calls) begins with Ozzie Smith's walk-off home run in Game Five of the 1985 National League Championship Series ("Go crazy folks! Go crazy!") and continues two days later in Game Six with Jack Clark's three-run home run ("Adios! Goodbye! And maybe, that's a winner!"). Others that followed include his call of the injured Kirk Gibson's dramatic game-winning pinch-hit home run in Game One of the 1988 World Series ("I don't believe what I just saw!"), and Kirby Puckett's game-winning home run in Game Six of the 1991 World Series ("And we'll see you tomorrow night!"). His simple refrain when Mark McGwire hit his record-tying 61st home run in 1998 came with a very innocent yet simple epitaph ("Pardon me while I stand up and applaud."). His summation of Bruce Sutter's final pitch of the 1982 World Series ("a swing and a miss! And that's a winner! That's a winner! A World Series winner for the Cardinals!") was later shortened to a simple "And that's a winner" to punctuate each Cardinal win and leave Cardinal fans with gentle assurance that things are alright in the world.

While Buck was "a winner" broadcasting baseball, he also became a winner behind the mic as the original voice of the National Hockey League's St. Louis Blues. His football coverage included two decades as the radio voice of Monday Night Football alongside Hank Stram, not to mention 17 Super Bowls, leading to his selection for the Pro Football Hall of Fame's Pete Rozelle Radio-Television Award in 1996.

Getty Images

Ford C. Frick Award Recipient—1987

Born: *August 21, 1924, in Holyoke, MO*

Died: *June 18, 2002, in St. Louis, MO*

Buried: *Jefferson Barracks National Cemetery in St. Louis, MO*

Major League Teams Broadcast: *St. Louis Cardinals (1954–1959, 1961–1971, 1976–2000)*

Harry Caray

For over a half century, Harry Caray was the baseball voice of the Midwest. Having risen from the streets of St. Louis under his given name Harry Carabina, Harry changed his surname to Caray after an early radio station manager felt that Carabina "sounded too awkward on the air." In 1945, Harry made it to the big leagues as a broadcaster for not one but two teams: St. Louis's Browns and Cardinals. While with the Cardinals, he would work with three other Ford Frick Award Winners: Jack Buck, Joe Garagiola, and Milo Hamilton. And it was in St. Louis that perhaps the proudest moment of his career occurred in 1958, as he was able to call the 3000th hit of his favorite player, Stan Musial.

Remembered as the announcer with the oversized black glasses, the catchphrase "Holy Cow," and for singing "Take Me Out to the Ballgame" during the seventh-inning stretch, Harry was quite different from the more sedate broadcasters of his era. He was unapologetically outspoken and opinionated—a trait that often did not sit well with the players he covered. But he was also an unquestioned salesman, selling his sponsors' beer, and selling whichever team he covered with an "unabashed homerism." Often these zealous traits led to a career marked with controversy.

Harry's national profile had risen dramatically during his coverage of three Cardinal World Series in the 1960s for NBC. His dismissal from the Redbirds' broadcast team at the owner's behest in 1969 was marked with intrigue and mystery over its reasoning.

Harry quickly rebounded with a one-season job broadcasting for the Oakland A's and their controversial owner Charlie Finley in 1970. A year later Harry headed back to the Midwest and landed on the shore of Lake Michigan working for the Chicago White Sox. He spent 11 seasons with the Sox before cementing his national profile by moving to Chicago's other team in 1982 to lead the Cubs' broadcast team on their evolving cable television superstation WGN. Sixteen years later and after 53 years in the broadcast booth, Caray unexpectedly passed away. He had never missed a single game in his first 41 seasons. There are two words that can rightly summarize his broadcast career, which covered over 8,300 big league games—Holy Cow.

Getty Images

Ford C. Frick Award Recipient—1989

Born: *March 1, 1914, in St. Louis, MO*

Died: *February 18, 1989, in Rancho Mirage, CA*

Major League Teams Broadcast: *St. Louis Browns (1945–1946), St. Louis Cardinals (1945–1969), Oakland Athletics (1970), Chicago White Sox (1971–1981), Chicago Cubs (1982–1997)*

Joe Garagiola

Joe Garagiola grew up on the same Italian neighborhood street in St. Louis as Yogi Berra. They spent their whole childhood together and remained lifelong friends. Despite their mutual love of baseball, they took different career paths within the game. Yogi would play 19 seasons in the big leagues, manage another seven, and play in 14 World Series. Joe became a journeyman catcher playing for four teams (Cardinals 1946–51, Pirates 1951–53, Cubs 1953–54, Giants 1954) and played in only one World Series (1946). Both would make it to Cooperstown—Yogi as a player and Joe as a broadcaster. Joe summed the situation up pretty well: "Not only was I not the best catcher in the major leagues, I wasn't even the best catcher on my street!"

It was that self-deprecating humor and a career batting average of .257 that sent Joe in a different direction. After Harry Caray recommended Joe join the Cardinals' broadcast team for Major League Baseball's largest radio network, Joe's popularity soared. His book, *Baseball is a Funny Game*, became a best seller. He was on NBC's *Tonight Show* and began doing segments on their *Today* show. Joe began working on the network's *Game of the Week* in 1961 before switching to the Yankees' broadcast booth in 1965 and then going back to the *Today* show in 1967. In 1974 Joe started a 15-year run behind the microphone for NBC's *Game of the Week*. He would later call games for the California Angeles and Arizona Diamondbacks before hosting the popular Westminster Kennel Club Dog Show. Joe humorously summarized his career as follows: "I played in the World Series, and I broadcast the World Series. I broadcast the All-Star Game. I've done the *Today* show, the *Tonight Show*, The Tomorrow Show, the Yesterday Show, the Day After Tomorrow Show." "And people come up to me and say, "I love you in Westminster."

Getty Images

Ford C. Frick Award Recipient—1991

Born: *February 12, 1926, in St. Louis, MO*

Died: *March 23, 2016, in Scottsdale, AZ*

Buried: *Resurrection Cemetery in St. Louis, MO*

Major League Teams Broadcast: *St. Louis Cardinals (1955–1962), New York Yankees (1965–1967), California Angels (1990), Arizona Diamondbacks (1998–2012)*

National Network Broadcasts: *NBC Game of the Week (1961–1964, 1974–1988)*

Milo Hamilton

With a signature line of "Holy Toledo," Milo Hamilton spent six decades calling MLB games for seven different teams. His career began in St. Louis and ended in Houston. In the booth, he shared the microphone with four other Ford Frick Award winners: Jack Brickhouse, Jack Buck, Harry Caray, and Bob Elson, delivering many of baseball's most memorable moments.

He was at the microphone when Hank Aaron became the all-time Home Run King in 1973. Twelve years earlier he had called Roger Maris's record-breaking 61st home run using a Western Union ticker. He would call Nolan Ryan's 4,000th strikeout along with 11 no-hitters—the most memorable being Mike Scott's season-ending, division-clinching "no-no" in 1986. As fate would have it, Hamilton was in the booth in 1954 when Stan Musial hit five home runs in a doubleheader and again 18 years later when the San Diego Padres Nate Colbert did the same.

Hamilton's MLB coverage began during the St. Louis Browns' final season in 1953. Instead of going to Baltimore with the team, he joined the Cardinals' broadcasts alongside Buck and Caray. Hamilton was let go after one season to make room for Joe Garagiola. He then teamed with Brickhouse, broadcasting Chicago Cubs games before being dismissed by club owner Phil Wrigley to make room for Lou Boudreau. Hamilton then spent time alongside White Sox announcer Elson before joining the Braves in their first season in Atlanta in 1966. Forced off the Braves crew after critical comments about the team's poor attendance, Hamilton headed to Pittsburgh to replace the retiring Bob Prince. Hamilton's style didn't mesh well there, so he rejoined the Cubs broadcast team—that is, until Harry Caray came on board. Hamilton always felt Caray had pushed him out of the Cardinals booth in 1956, and the relationship again forced Hamilton out once more in 1984. Hamilton, however, bounced back the next year and found a longtime home behind the microphone of the Houston Astros on his way to Cooperstown.

St. Louis Browns Historical Society

Ford C. Frick Award Recipient—1992
Born: *September 2, 1927, in Fairfield, IA*
Died: *September 17, 2015, in Houston, TX*
Buried: *Cremated*
Major League Teams Broadcast: *St. Louis Browns (1953), St. Louis Cardinals (1954), Chicago Cubs (1956–57, 1980–84), Chicago White Sox (1962–65), Atlanta Braves (1966–75), Pittsburgh Pirates (1976–79), Houston Astros (1985–2012)*

Tim McCarver

Tim McCarver's seven decades in baseball began on the playing field and ended in the broadcast booth. As a player he was a champion. As an announcer he was an award-winner. His big-league playing career began with the St. Louis Cardinals in 1959, one month shy of his 18th birthday. The two-time World Series champion's 21-season playing career touched four decades. He caught two of his era's best pitchers in Bob Gibson and Steve Carlton, and he was behind the plate for many of their record-setting accomplishments. By the time his career ended with the Philadelphia Phillies in 1980, McCarver had played in three World Series (1964, 1967, 1968) and two All-Star Games (1966, 1967). In 1967 he was runner-up to Cardinal teammate Orlando Cepeda in the N.L. MVP race. McCarver also played a role in helping the Phillies to three consecutive N.L. Championship Series (1976, 1977, 1978) before announcing his retirement after the 1979 season.

During the 1980 season, McCarver joined the Philadelphia Phillies' radio broadcasting team but came out of retirement to play in six games for the team that went on to win the World Series. Those games pushed him into his fourth decade on the field. His 21 seasons as a player would be followed by four decades in the broadcast booth. He continued broadcasting Phillies games for the next two seasons before working more nationally televised games during his years with the New York Mets and Yankees. Nationally, McCarver broadcast ABC's *Monday Night Baseball* games with Jim Palmer and Al Michaels. At CBS, his broadcast partner was Jack Buck, whose son Joe Buck would become McCarver's future partner on the Fox Network. When McCarver backed away from the spotlight of national games, he returned to his original roots in baseball in St. Louis, broadcasting Cardinals baseball for six seasons. During his tenure in the booth, McCarver was able to use his experiences on the field to offer insights and observations so those watching or listening better enjoyed the game.

Getty Images

Ford C. Frick Award Recipient—2012

Born: *October 16, 1941, in Memphis, TN*

Died: *February 16, 2023, in Memphis, TN*

Buried: *Cremated*

Major League Teams Broadcast: *Philadelphia Phillies (1980–1982), New York Mets (1983–1998), New York Yankees (1999–2001), San Fransisco Giants (2002), St. Louis Cardinals (2014–2019)*

National Network Broadcasts: *ABC Monday Night Baseball (1984–1989), CBS Baseball (1992–1993), Fox Baseball (1996–2013)*

BBWAA Career Excellence Award Winners—Sportswriters

The BBWAA Career Excellence Award, formerly known as the J.G. Taylor Spink Award, is the highest award given by the Baseball Writers' Association of America (BBWAA). It is given "for meritorious contributions to baseball writing." The winners of the award are not members of the Hall of Fame in Cooperstown, New York. They are not "inducted" or "enshrined." They are not "Hall of Fame sportswriters," and there is no "writers' wing" of the Hall of Fame. But winners are permanently recognized in an exhibit at the Hall of Fame's library.

The award was created in 1962 and named after St. Louisan J.G. Taylor Spink following his death. Spink had been the publisher of The Sporting News from 1914 to 1962, and he would be the award's first recipient. In February 2021, the BBWAA voted to remove his name from the award "due to Spink's troubled history in supporting segregated baseball."

The BBWAA is a professional association for journalists writing about Major League Baseball for daily newspapers, magazines, and qualifying websites. The organization was founded in 1908. In addition to bestowing this award, its members vote annually on candidates for the National Baseball Hall of Fame, as well as the Most Valuable Player, Cy Young, Rookie of the Year, Manager of the Year, and Edgar Martinez (designated hitter) awards each year.

J.G. Taylor Spink

J.G. Taylor Spink was honored as the first recipient of the J.G. Taylor Spink Award in 1962 following his passing. In 2021 the award's name was changed to the Baseball Writers' Association of America Career Excellence Award. Spink received the award in recognition of his near half-century of work publishing *The Sporting News*. His uncle, Alfred Spink, began the weekly publication on March 17, 1886. Met with great acclaim, it soon had the highest circulation of any sports publication west of Philadelphia. Taylor's father Charles (Alfred's brother) began running the publication in 1890 and ran it until his passing in 1914, when Taylor Spink became its owner and publisher.

As the sport of baseball was grabbing the nation's attention, *The Sporting News* quenched the nation's thirst for information. Under Taylor Spink's leadership *The Sporting News* brought baseball's highlights from across the nation to fans through weekly printed updates about the players, the games, and the pennant races. *The Sporting News* became known across the nation as the "baseball bible." It further disseminated baseball stories through publications like the annual *Record Book* (dating back to the early 1900s) and the *Baseball Register* (first produced in 1940). The newspaper also began handing out awards every year, with the most prestigious being *The Sporting News'* Player of the Year Award.

Through his hard-fisted drive and genius, Taylor Spink made his St. Louis office and *The Sporting News* the epicenter of baseball information. Taylor Spink's life and publications were acclaimed throughout the "golden years" of baseball. It was a time when there was no immediate access through the 24-hour sports cycles of cable television or the Internet. In 1969 Spink was inducted into the National Sports Media Association's Hall of Fame. His biography for the award ceremony summarizes the impact he made on baseball with the statement, "Spink was so important to baseball that it is said, if Taylor Spink had not existed, organized baseball would have been forced to invent him."

While the publication continued to be a beacon of baseball long after his passing, Taylor Spink's name was removed from the baseball writing award in 2021 after researchers identified issues within publications printed prior to baseball's integration in 1947. Those findings exposed racist language, ugly stereotypes, and derogatory portrayals of Negro League players and other African Americans during Spink's time.

Getty Images

BBWAA Career Excellence Award—1962
Born: *November 6, 1888, in St, Louis, MO*
Died: *December 7, 1962, in Clayton, MO*
Buried: *Bellefontaine Cemetery, St. Louis, MO*
Major League Coverage: *The Sporting News*

J. Roy Stockton

J. Roy Stockton's first coverage of baseball was not about a major league team but rather the Federal League's 1915 St. Louis Terriers. However, his name would soon become synonymous with Major League Baseball through his coverage of the St. Louis Cardinals.

Stockton joined the *St. Louis Post-Dispatch* in 1917. He became the newspaper's beat writer covering the Cardinals and later became the paper's sports editor in 1946. The decades between the start of Stockton's career and his retirement in 1958 were some of the most exciting years in St. Louis baseball. The Cardinals won nine N.L. pennants and six World Championships. The Browns also won an A.L. pennant during that period.

The eyes of the nation's baseball fans remained focused on the St. Louis baseball scene and the man who typed its stories. But Stockton did more than just write for his hometown newspaper. In the early 1930s he became one of the ghostwriters for Christy Walsh's publications officially authored by famous athletes. He wrote many of the articles published under Dizzy Dean's byline. He also wrote a series of baseball profiles in *The Saturday Evening Post* during the heyday of the Cardinals' "Gas House Gang." The articles were subsequently published as two books, *The Gas House Gang* and *A Couple of Other Guys.*

Stockton's baseball coverage was not limited to just the written word. In 1947, he appeared in St. Louis's first broadcast of a local baseball game on television station KSDK-TV and hosted an evening sports radio program for 15 years. His 1932 selection as the president of the BBWAA, the consideration for the job of Major League Baseball's Commissioner in 1951, and his place as a member of the Hall of Fame's Veterans Committee provide some evidence of his stature in the game. Another of his lasting gifts to St. Louis baseball was his hiring of his successor, Bob Broeg.

St. Louis Media History Archive

BBWAA Career Excellence Award—1972

Born: *December 16, 1892, in St, Louis, MO*

Died: *August 24, 1972, in St, Petersburg, FL*

Buried: *Not identified*

Major League Coverage: *The St. Louis Post–Dispatch (1917–1958)*

Bob Broeg

Growing up in his native St. Louis, Bob Broeg became an avid writer for his school's newspaper and yearbook while spending his summers playing sports and working odd jobs to afford tickets to Browns or Cardinals games. In his youth he was already covering sports. He helped the *St. Louis Post-Dispatch*'s prep sports editor cover high school games and even became a ticket-taker at Sportsman's Park so he could watch baseball games for free. Broeg attended the University of Missouri's School of Journalism, where he continued writing for the school's newspaper and the Associated Press (AP). He stayed with the AP after his graduation in 1940 before joining the *St. Louis Star–Times* in 1942. With America at war, Broeg joined the Marines and returned from service in 1945 to land his dream job in the sports department of the *St. Louis Post–Dispatch*.

There Broeg adopted his trademark look—the bow tie—simply because it looked better and traveled better while on the move tracking down stories. The beat he really wanted was the Cardinals, but that was held by BBWAA Award winner J. Roy Stockton, so Broeg covered the Browns. While the Browns didn't have the pedigree of the Cardinals, they provided Broeg with many special stories. Trading drinks with owner Bill Veeck one August evening in 1951, Broeg was told to have a photographer at the next day's doubleheader. Broeg didn't know what would happen, but that tidbit of information landed him the iconic story and photo of three-foot seven-inch Eddie Gaedel's sole at-bat in the major leagues. A year later Broeg got his dream job covering the Cardinals and spent the next four decades highlighting stories from his beloved team for St. Louis and the nation. One such story led to Stan Musial forever becoming Stan "The Man," as Broeg wrote about the Brooklyn Dodger fans labeling the Cardinal each time, he came to the plate with the cry from the stands "here comes that man."

As the stories continued to come from his typewriter, Broeg's esteem rose as well. In 1958 he was elected President of the BBWAA. He became deeply involved with the Baseball Hall of Fame and was named to its Board of Directors in 1972, where he served for 28 years guiding the legacy of baseball. Even after he officially retired, he continued writing Sunday columns for the paper and hosting a KMOX radio show while churning out many books on sports.

Wikimedia Commons

BBWAA Career Excellence Award—1979
Born: *March 18, 1918, in St, Louis, MO*
Died: *October 28, 2005, in St, Louis, MO*
Buried: *Sunset Memorial Park, Affton, MO*
Major League Coverage: *St. Louis Star–Times (1942), St. Louis Post-Dispatch (1945–1987)*

Rick Hummel

Just like baseball's famous poem highlighting the legendary double-play combination of "Tinkers to Evers to Chance," St. Louisans could have a refrain highlighting the city's legendary sportswriters. The exhortation of "Stockton to Broeg to Hummel" would highlight the men of the *St. Louis Post-Dispatch* who daily quenched the thirst of generations of St. Louis's baseball loving fans. These three men formed a chain of over 100 years of continuous baseball coverage.

Like his mentor Bob Broeg, who hired him, Hummel graduated from the University of Missouri's School of Journalism and joined the sports department staff of the *Post-Dispatch* after spending time in the military. Once on the job, Hummel began covering various sports before covering his first Cardinal game in 1973. He became the Cardinals' beat writer in 1978. During his 51 years at the *Post-Dispatch* Hummel covered 42 consecutive MLB All-Star Games, seven Cardinal N.L. pennants, and their three World Series Championships as a writer and columnist before his retirement after the 2022 season. His subjects in print comprise many of baseball's greatest in the era of his coverage of the game. It's a list of Hall of Famers that begins with Lou Brock and flows through Ozzie Smith and future Hall of Famer Albert Pujols. He documented them all, and he also covered three of the Cardinals' managers (Joe Torre, Whitey Herzog, and Tony La Russa) whose plaques now hang in Cooperstown.

Hummel was nicknamed "Commish," short for "The Commissioner," for running an APBA board game league with colleagues over the years and enforcing the play of the games with his encyclopedic knowledge of baseball, its rules, its players, and its history. In 1994 he was selected to serve as president of the BBWAA. Hummel became a a long-time member of the Hall of Fame's Overview Committee, which reviews the careers of potential inductees by the Veterans Committee. In recognition for all he gave to the game, the press box of the Cardinals' Busch Stadium III is now named after him.

BBWAA Career Excellence Award—2006
Born: *February 25, 1946, in Quincy, IL*
Died: *May 20, 2023, in St, Louis, MO*
Buried: *Not identified*
Major League Coverage: *St. Louis Post-Dispatch (1971–2022)*

Index

★ ★